PAZAZZ

PAZAZZ

THE IMPACT AND RESONANCE
OF WHITE CLOTHING

Nina Edwards

REAKTION BOOKS

For P.A.H.

Published by
Reaktion Books Ltd
Unit 32, Waterside
44–48 Wharf Road
London N1 7UX, UK
www.reaktionbooks.co.uk

First published 2023
Copyright © Nina Edwards 2023

Printed and bound in Great Britain by
TJ Books Ltd, Padstow, Cornwall

A catalogue record for this book is available from the British Library

ISBN 978 1 78914 685 1

Contents

Introduction *7*

ONE The Ancient Gods of Fashion *17*

TWO The Spiritual, the Professional
and the Uniform *29*

THREE Fashionable Men, Veils and Gloves *53*

FOUR Powdered Wigs and Muslins *79*

FIVE Underwear and Dirt *125*

SIX Meringues and Sleek Satin Shifts *147*

SEVEN High Fashion and Street Fashion *159*

EIGHT Whiteout *185*

References *197*

Bibliography *211*

Acknowledgements *216*

Photo Acknowledgements *217*

Index *218*

Quantities of white cloth draped on fences to dry in the sun,
Delhi, India, 1978, photograph by Theodore D. Goldfarb.

Introduction

White is always in fashion. Put simply, it impresses. It beguiles and demands attention and stands in the face of practicality. And it can be ordinary too. In the colour spectrum both white and black are absent, and yet without the presence of a degree of white light we cannot experience colour at all. It is vulnerable to accident, but in these days of stay-at-home fashion with the emphasis on comfort, to reach for a white serge coat or linen shirt can be an act of defiance.

In the history of dress, white clothing has been an indicator of aspiration and wealth. Rules such as white not being suitable for seasons other than spring and summer are now largely ignored.[1] There was a time when few would have worn something so easily soiled and requiring such frequent washing, if they hoped to avoid looking shabby. To wear white was to demonstrate that you did not have to do your own laundry. Today wearing a jacket in virgin white wool, for example, at the very least suggests you can afford regular trips to a dry cleaner.

Our attitudes to dress are sometimes revealed through details that we might think hardly concern us, yet when an attribute seems wrong, we can feel challenged and uneasy. The first time being treated by a nurse in coloured scrubs or watching cricket played in fluorescent nylon, or tennis with the players in dark form-fitting neoprene, can induce a sense that something has been lost or is perhaps missing. Coco Chanel's biographer Claude Delay describes the billowing dress

Religious procession of the Fete-Dieu au Jardin, with nuns
and first communicants at the Hotel Dieu de Beaune, *c.* 1930.

Miniature brides of Christ: a First Holy Communion
at the Loreto Convent Msongari, Nairobi, 1963.

and veil Chanel wore to her First Communion as being 'the first dress, the most important dress, the dress that made her a couturière'.[2] I recall my delight in wearing a shiny Tricel frock and veil for my own First Communion, and the pain of the white patent-leather ballerina pumps, half a size too small. A few years later I was ashamed of the clothing I wore for my Confirmation – all white, but now it was an old school tennis skirt, woollen sports jumper and plimsolls, my mother's ideas having moved on. It felt all wrong. The itchiness of the jumper and even the familiar everyday comfort of the shoes made me despair for my shallow soul. Then I took my religion seriously, and this peevish longing for finery, for excess, seemed shameful, though now I am not so sure. One thing was clear: there was white clothing and white clothing and, right or wrong, I knew which I preferred.

What does it mean to wear white? Is there something about white clothing that has special symbolic meaning and, if so, how much of this comes from the bodily experience of wearing white? White cloth has historically been difficult to attain and difficult to maintain, impractical and easily stained. When it is grubby it conjures up very different associations. It has become a cliché to say it denotes cleanliness, innocence and purity, but it can also suggest class superiority

Ku Klux Klan, 1922.

and privilege, aspiration and, on occasion, hope. Not to mention style and fine, frivolous verve. It represents the menace of Ku Klux Klan anonymity. A fan of the multi-ethnic funk band War wore a Klan outfit to one of their concerts, in 1979. It made wearing a nightdress and conical hat as a threat seem comically absurd. It can mark the transition of a bride to the married state, as if her costume cleanses her of the past; it can be appropriate dress for mourning and for shrouds, palls and ghosts. When white garments are elegantly refined, in fine linen, soft cashmere, liquid silk satin or delicate handmade lace, they can denote conspicuous expense; however, the straitjacket in contrast is tough stuff. Sewn from old sails and proofed with stinking fat and tallow, it indicates the loss of individual freedom. In women's dress, in the West in particular, white clothing has been a marker of an affluent, leisured life; in men's dress it is often subtle evidence of control in the discreet and pristine framing of dark, business-like masculine uniformity. When on occasion all-white garb is worn by men, it can register both control and servility. In the 1980s, for instance, IBM's male office staff were told they had to be clean-shaven and wear white shirts as part of their corporate identity. It was a strategy designed to avoid offending their customers, white suggesting a neutral conformism. White can be a startling, attention-seeking absence of colour, glam-orously stylish, sometimes threatening but in other more everyday contexts modestly plain – and rarely perhaps, but quite simply, a thing of beauty. Coco Chanel claimed that the popularity of white in Paris after the economic crash of 1929 answered a post-traumatic need for 'candid innocence and white satin'.[3]

Within the wide range of meanings that white inhabits, in the contentious ground where clothing is read as a series of signs, then white is the opposite of black in meaning as it is in hue. Two monochrome 'non-colour' colours, they vie for dominance. *Pazazz* unravels the complex metaphor of white garments – a subject that has largely been ignored compared with the attention given to black. The term 'pazazz' was coined by Diana Vreeland, editor of American *Vogue* in the 1960s, to evoke the spirit and glamour of fashion, and is adopted here to suggest the peculiar allure of white clothing, from early undyed cloth and wrapped clothing to the astounding finesse of

Satin and tulle reflecting light in movie-star glamour, 1937,
photograph by Wynn Richards.

couture fashion, through the ages and in many different cultures. It can suggest the badge of respectability of a modest white shirt, or the ubiquitous plain white T-shirt and cheap but spotless white trainers. Whiteness holds its ground. The eye is drawn towards light and white reflects light most effectively, and so it follows that it has often been the choice for high-status clothing, drawing attention to the wearer. In the context of design, its effect can be cleanly uncompromising. The modern availability and affordability of bleached white cloth might lead one to expect a lessening of this impact, but this is not so. Its value persists.

The history of wearing white influences attitudes to its use in fashion today, even in the many cases when we may not consider that fashion is at all relevant. The attention afforded to black clothing, for men especially, has meant that its white opposite tends to be mentioned only in passing. It is as if black had more gravitas and therefore deserves more of our notice, white being considered more ephemeral, transient and even trite. While many in the West adopt

Servants need to look impeccably clean if they are to be hired:
Charles-François Marchal, *The Servants' Fair at Bouxwiller*, 1864, oil on canvas.

View of the Casbah, rue Kléber, Algiers,
1876–90, photograph by Alexandre Leroux.

dark clothing as a flattering, would-be sophisticated and perhaps easy
neutral choice, white is both rarer and often more highly valued. True
to its Janus-like nature, to some it suggests vulgarity, associated with
too much bare flesh, fake tan or bling jewellery, demonstrating a lack
of refined style. In the history of dress, white has also been a marker
of subtlety, sometimes modest discretion, and conversely its absence
has been an indication of poverty. When worn by wives or servants,
as by a maid dressed in an impeccable cap and apron, it is a sign of
their servility. The fact that it is hard to maintain makes it strangely
suitable for the formal effect required of various uniforms, civil and
military. For Western men, despite the late eighteenth-century Great
Male Renunciation of Colour in male dress,[4] dark clothing across all
levels of society still required the contrasting whiteness of a pristine
linen shirt to achieve respectability. Today the white business shirt,
even if worn tieless or merely represented by a spotless white T-shirt,

remains a signifier of a serious-minded, professional attitude. For the traditionally dressed Arab man, his long white robes must also be seen to be unsoiled. To wear white in both spheres is to show that you do not concern yourself with menial, physically strenuous work and demonstrates one's position over those that do.

White clothing has been adopted as a uniform by scientists, doctors and nurses, and other specific roles such as cook, baker and house painter. A chef's whites are worn not only to denote cleanliness but as a mark of pride and status. The double-breasted jacket, as worn by Marie-Antoine Carême, can be reversed to hide stains during a service; the tall white hat or toque, introduced by Auguste Escoffier, is said to allow the head to cool in a sweltering kitchen. The higher the toque, the more important the chef. Where non-white uniforms are adopted in the kitchen, they tend to be or include black, the alternative non-colour colour. White cotton suits and pith helmets were worn in the Raj by British officials and all-white clothing by their families, and often by their servants. Surprisingly, while white clothing does not absorb as much light as dark clothing, it reflects body radiation back to the body, which black does not. However, we tend to believe that white and paler colours will keep us cool. The white safari-style uniform sometimes known as tropical whites was first worn by the British during the Second Boer War in South Africa. It finds its modern-day expression in shirt-like jackets with external pleated pockets, in the fashions of the 1960s and '70s, as worn by Roger Moore as James Bond himself – dapper in cream silk in *The Man with the Golden Gun* (1974) – and more generally in the staple white or buff linen blazer. In some armed forces white or buff – a near-white that does not quite so easily show the dirt – is used for summer uniform and sometimes for elegant evening garb on the smartest of occasions. In postcolonial India the safari suit is still worn by public servants. However, in the political sphere, ever since Mahatma Gandhi took to wearing a white khadi cotton dhoti and shawl in the 1920s, others have followed his example, wearing undyed homespun cloth to identify themselves with the rural poor. Dipesh Chakrabarty describes undyed khadi cloth as a symbol of simplicity and poverty, and, in relation to those of some status, as carrying the suggestion of self-sacrifice.[5] The practice underlies a deep-seated fear of bodily corruption, white clothing signalling both physical and moral incorruptibility. Imran Khan, former prime minister of Pakistan (2018–22), tended to avoid the Western-style clothing of his cricketing past. In September 2021 he wore his signature white shalwar kameez and black square-cut waistcoat with Nehru collar for a meeting with the Saudi crown prince, the latter in a voluminous tribal white gown with a woven gold border. Reham Khan has also come to favour traditional clothing, and is often pictured with a filmy white lawn dupatta shawl draped elegantly over her head, a symbol of modesty in both India and Pakistan.

So, white is widespread, through history and across many cultures, its meaning complex but united by the impact and resonance of a light-filled absence of colour. When white seems too stark it can be dimmed or enriched, from off-white to cream, ivory to translucent pearl.

Standing draped woman, *c.* 300 BCE, terracotta sculpture
with traces of paint, the colour almost entirely worn away.

ONE

The Ancient Gods
of Fashion

Vestis virum facit. Clothes make the man.
To dress within the formal limits and with an air gives men,
as the Greek line testifies, authority.
Erasmus quoting the *Institutions* of Quintilian,
who is in turn citing Homer

Across the River Thames from Kew Gardens in West London, and surveying the mysterious gardens of Syon Park, the statue of Flora, goddess of flowers and of spring, stands atop an 18 metre (60 ft) Doric column, gazing out towards the lake as she casts seed upon the ground. She appears to be wearing a plain white linen Roman toga. It is difficult to get an accurate picture of what exactly was worn in ancient civilizations, particularly when investigating something as ephemeral as colour in dress. We may think that we already know the meaning of white clothing and search only for confirmation of our views. Looking at the ancient past via our understanding of more recent times runs the risk, as with the overconfident scientist determined to confirm a hypothesis, of ascribing values to whiteness or paleness that we feel we already know are true.

Since ancient descriptions in relation to colour are rare, there is scarce evidence to test our suppositions. There are, however, some contemporary written accounts, and there exist also the wealth of artefacts: the wall paintings, statuary, illustrated vases and terracottas of the ancient world. In ancient Egypt, because of the dry climate and the conditions within the pyramids, actual clothing belonging to those of high status and their servants does remain. In contrast, the more temperate climate of ancient Greece, together with Athenian cremation practices, means that no garments have been found, and what was once thought to be ancient Greek clothing has turned out to be more recent. More generally, cloth that may once have been brilliantly dyed can easily become faded with time and bleached of colour, and then mistakenly thought to have been originally white or at least pale in hue. Moreover, ancient artists may have exaggerated contrasts in colour for the integrity of their work, so we should be wary of assuming that their records of the styles of the day are entirely accurate. Vases depicting figures dressed in black must be seen in the context of the fashion for black relief work, and the same may be true in relation to white figures in relief against a dark background. In like manner, statues honoured for their pristine marble whiteness in modern times have been shown to have originally been colourfully painted, the features of body and dress having merely worn away, leading us to believe they were always elegantly colour-free.

Yet, while these provisos must be borne in mind, our knowledge of the clothing of the ancient past, although limited and sometimes mistaken, still provides some perspective on the personal and social identities of those distant times. Moreover, in our imaginations classical clothing is largely white, albeit conjured from the limited evidence available and hampered by our various prejudices, and in turn reflects light onto contemporary habits of dress.

We look to remaining aboriginal people to understand what was worn before the first crafted cloth – animal skins and larger, durable leaves to provide warmth and protection – their clothing, in the evidence of cut and detail, expressing our deep-seated desire for the aesthetic which is at the birth of fashion. It may seem an ordinary enough study to investigate what was worn. Yet such small beginnings, since we all wear clothes and have decided views about what we do and do not like, may have something to say about how we live and what matters most to us. There is an old riddle concerning what

Adam and Eve, detail from the Sarcophagus of Junius Bassus,
359 CE, marble, St Peter's Basilica, Vatican City.

clothing Adam and Eve could possibly have put on after their fall
from grace, to cover their sudden awareness of and shame at their
nakedness. They are sometimes depicted cowering in loincloths, yet
how would this have been possible? What would have been available
to them in the Garden of Eden? The answer, of course, is snakeskin,
sloughed from the body of the Devil incarnate. No wonder, one might
argue, the bad press fashion receives in the West. We shroud ourselves
in the silvery skin of original sinfulness, in Satan's skin.

Sin aside, there is pleasure to be had in clothing ourselves. We may
be ashamed of our naked bodies or simply want to protect ourselves
from the elements, but even those who profess to have no interest at
all in what they wear may be appalled to wear garments that seem

inappropriate or expose them to ridicule. My father was a careless dresser, and would have considered it unmanly to be otherwise, yet he was careful to turn out neatly in a suit for a funeral or other occasions that required respectful formality. A friend who is seldom seen in anything but jeans and a sweatshirt nonetheless turned up to my father's funeral in a neat skirt. In like manner, many women, not confident of their appearance or ability to take centre stage, still feel it right and proper to wed in white. Clothing matters to us all.

The first clothing, the first manufactured cloth, would have been undyed, relying on the natural hue of linen or wool, yet even then what was whitest among the creams, greys and beiges must have stood out. Across Scandinavia cloth dyeing came later than in southern Europe, variety relying instead on the wide range of natural colours in wool. Dyed cloth has been discovered from as early as the Bronze Age, the Egyptians using iron oxide and the Mesopotamians vegetable dyes such as sumac from before the end of the third millennium. In Britain there is evidence of coloured dyes being used from the first century BCE. And yet the pure whiteness of cloth has always been an end in itself: the ancient Persians, for example, believed that all gods wore white, and in most religions, where gods are depicted, they tend to be robed in white.

Ancient Egyptians believed that fabrics derived from animals were unclean and forbade them in religious places, generally favouring plant-derived linen, which was cool and lightweight and therefore pleasant against the skin in their hot dry climate. It seems from wall and ceramic art that nobles appeared to dress largely in white, Old Kingdom Egyptians in particular wearing clothes that were wholly white, like the sacred mummies and Isis herself. The pharaohs are depicted in white crowns, a loincloth, a tunic or simple shirt and, during the Middle Kingdom period, a stiffly pleated white skirt or kilt. Though there are sometimes bands of colour on the translucent linen, matching the colourful jewellery worn by both sexes, it is the adherence to white cloth by pharaohs and their near relations that associates them with deities. Therefore white cloth suggests piety as well as purity. In like manner, for other lesser but still powerful classes, it would have been important to dress in non-colours to associate

Cypriot male votary statuette, early 6th century BCE, limestone.

themselves with the highest echelons of society. Expensive to produce, fine linen could reveal the body beneath, or the presence of inner layers of fine clothing, particularly in New Kingdom fashion. Women's clothing shows less stylistic changes, the upper classes wearing narrow white shifts. Higher classes of women wore longer skirts. These skirts were sometimes held in place by colourful woven braces, worn over the shoulder or between naked breasts. In contrast, slaves of both genders were often naked apart perhaps from a loincloth of undyed coarse linen. One might say that the powerless had no choice but to be unclothed, whereas the more powerful chose to reveal themselves through the medium of luxuriously transparent materials, sometimes suggestively veiled yet often deliberately exposing breast and flank.

Although there was a considerable knowledge of dyeing techniques in the Middle Period, coloured clothing was associated with foreigners:

> In Egyptian art foreigners, particularly 'Asiatics' and servants (who may themselves have been foreign slaves), wore coloured and patterned garments which emphasize their barbarity in contrast to the fine bleached linens worn by Egyptians.[1]

Sculpture of Cleopatra in an intricately folded and pleated gown,
William Wetmore Story, 1858, carved 1869, marble.

Could it be that, by wearing a purple himation mantle, Mark Antony unwittingly lessened his status in the eyes of the powerful of Egypt, making him seem more the barbarian interloper, despite his white Roman toga?[2]

Minoan priests and priestesses wore white garments made of linen and wool, and these represent the first evidence of sewn garments, which gave a better fit than wrapped clothing. There was also a belief in the importance of cleanliness, which could be best expressed with white clothing, since a soiled outer appearance might suggest the nature of the inner man.[3] In Athenian culture, despite the widely held impression that citizens wore white exclusively, colour was sometimes worn. Moreover, the scholar and archaeologist Maria Millington Evans, writing on ancient Greek dress, makes the general point that the Greek empire encompassed a wide range of cultures, from the military ideals of Sparta to the 'grace without softness' of Athens.[4] Women wore white veils, described by Homer as 'white and shining', made of linen, since wool would have been too heavy, and symbolizing feminine grace and affluence.[5] Silk would have rarely been available, and cotton tended only to be used for wadding rather than for weaving into cloth. Men also wore white as a mark of their status: 'These white garments were frequently cleaned by the fuller, their spotlessness being a test of good breeding. Workmen and field labourers wore grey or brown.'[6]

In ancient Greece, the plain white or unbleached woollen himation was worn draped over the left shoulder and under the right. The toga, worn over the chiton tunic or often on its own, was difficult to arrange correctly round the body, particularly without the use of a brooch or pin. How well this was done marked the elegance and status of the wearer. Glenys Davies, a scholar of classical art, compares the correct manner of wearing the Roman toga to knowing how to tie one's bow-tie correctly.[7] Moreover, keeping it in place required a careful upright carriage, a distinction similarly marking one's class confidence perhaps. Women from wealthier Roman households wore more constraining garments, meaning that their dress could more easily become grubby where it rubbed against the body, and the difficulty of keeping it looking clean was again a reason white was an indicator of class.

Statue of man with an elaborately arranged Roman toga
draped over the left shoulder, 50–100 CE, marble.

The fold marks in clothing were also important in distinguishing what was either new or at least freshly laundered.[8] A 'man's character and culture were judged from its fold.'[9] Seneca the Younger takes a somewhat different view:

> I do not like . . . a garment bright from a small chest . . . nor one pressed by weights and a thousand tortures to force it to be splendid . . . but (I prefer) a house-garment of little value that has neither been watched over nor selected with care.[10]

Seneca's outlook was, on the whole, rare. It was freshness and evidence of pressing that were generally valued, or at least the appearance of such, since in order to maintain sparkling white garments, bleaching in the sun was often insufficient. Stained and dirty garments had to be not only rubbed with chalk and fumigated with sulphur but trampled by slaves' feet. Stale urine was the final recourse, used as a whitening agent for the toughest of stains. White clothing must have emanated what the classicist Kelly Olson rightly dubs the 'bad smell of status'.[11] Fresh water for laundry was at any rate often hard to come by when drinking water had to be the priority. Some were so disgusted by the processes required to maintain whiteness that they opted to leave their garments unwashed, creating a more familiar pull between conspicuous apparent cleanliness or newness, in our own time suggesting the new and crude, and the more subtle distinctions of grubby class and possibly shabby chic. In the nineteenth century, while it was considered by many that a respectable servant had to be unsoiled and thus cleanly dressed, this did not necessarily apply to their employers, who, depending on their status, might be at liberty to be slovenly in their habits if they so wished. A parallel in our own time might be applied to someone with chemically-whitened teeth set against an elderly person in old but finely tailored tweeds and worn brogues, their frayed collar and cuffs adding to the impression of rarefied dress. The higher-class purity and impracticality of white clothing in antiquity, initially a sign of superiority, eventually came to be seen as a feature of exaggerated effeminacy,[12] and an indicator of unseen filth and stench.

In Rome, a girl born of an affluent family wore white exclusively until she was married, the *toga praetexta* standing for her virginity. For her wedding she wore a straight white tunic, the *tunica recta*, but with a brightly coloured scarf and shoes suggesting her new role in marriage. Young women brought to Rome because of foreign conquests often retained their native, more colourful attire, sometimes as slave prostitutes, so that white clothing in contrast became associated with citizen women. In older women, while the cloak or himation might be dyed, the tunic or chiton beneath were more often white, denoting their womanly but unassailable position. Evans makes the point that

Homer's description of women's veils suggests that they must have been made of linen, as wool would not have reflected light.

Vestal priestesses' white robes represented purity, loyalty and chastity. While spinning and weaving were women's tasks, the classicist Marina Fischer describes an important distinction in ancient Greece between the roles of respectable married and lower-class (often prostitute) women.[13] While a citizen wife would spin and weave cloth at her leisure and could take considerable care and pride in its quality, those in different circumstances might be more constrained, with prostitutes often being forced by their brothel keepers to work on small frame looms in-between customers in order to supplement their income: 'Brothel slaves were forced to labour both as prostitutes and as wool-workers, and seemed to have worked wool on a greater scale than smaller establishments or independent free prostitutes.'[14]

Given the necessity for a female citizen to protect her position, she would have been loath to be represented in the suggestive settings and revealing clothing of many vase paintings. Fischer suggests that such depictions are much more likely to have been of prostitutes. The headdresses and net snoods we have come to associate with women's ancient Greek fashion might thus, it follows, have suggested the foreign and the prostitute to a contemporary eye.

The cloth-producing roles, contrasting the good and careful wife with the needs of the prostitute, set Athena the goddess of wool-working against Aphrodite the goddess of erotic love. Thus it is touching that there is substantial evidence of the dedications and offerings made to Athena by the working prostitutes of ancient Greece.[15] While prostitutes tended to produce small items that were better suited to their working circumstances, married women could create one-off garments, with sufficient cloth being made for the project underway and no more. The convenience of producing longer lengths of cloth to make further clothing, Evans suggests, was alien. Most of this work, whether done by wife or prostitute, was undertaken using wool, since the wearing of linen was thought to suggest oriental effeminacy.[16]

All Roman citizens wore white, especially on public occasions, with boys, who came of age at fourteen, giving up their *toga praetexta* and donning the white *toga virilis*, with its red band around the hem.

Men taking part in the Olympic Games were naked but wore a large cloak, or *chlamys*, white but again bordered with colour. Roman citizens seeking political office wore white robes brightened with chalk, the *stola candida*, hence our term 'candidate', and intended to represent their unblemished suitability. Indeed, before the end of the Republic, Octavian attempted to use clothing as a means of control, making it illegal for a citizen to enter the Forum without wearing the white toga, 'establishing clothing as an integral feature of Imperial iconography'.[17] As the Republic approached its end, there was a growing popularity for leggings or trousers in darker, practical hues, representing 'precisely the garments that once marked the barbarian'.[18] Cicero remarks in a letter to Atticus that he does not approve of Epicrates' leggings, even though they were white.[19] There were, moreover, vested interests in maintaining the conspicuous impracticality of white clothing, dark fabric needing less upkeep:

> since the fullers were accustomed to wash stains from white clothing (*albarum vestium*), and there would be no need of their services if people wore black clothing (*atris vestibus*), Varro said very neatly that the fullers feared the owl because mourning drove them to poverty.[20]

Kelly Olson suggests that white may have taken on ritual significance 'because of the difficulty and expense of rendering material white: some wool was naturally white, of course, but to get cloth white cost time and money, and the results were not permanent', as if the effort involved gave it added spiritual value.[21] White clothing would be deliberately dirtied by the family and friends of a man accused of a capital crime, the *vestes sordidae*, intending to induce pity. Conversely the expense of keeping white clothing white could be part of its cachet, the majority of white togas worn in practice being off-white and often grubby. Fullers treated cloth with chalk, kaolin and lime to produce a brilliant white and softened its texture with sulphur and clay, but the process had to be kept up regularly, a symbol of purity in effect relying on artificial staining and bleaching to achieve its appearance. In effect the role white clothing played in antiquity was complex, 'a conceptual device, not just an ornament of style'.[22]

Our ideas about ancient dress during the great civilizations of Egypt, Greece and Rome continue to influence white clothing today, and its significance, however muddled and inaccurate, has remained. From the late eighteenth century into the nineteenth in the United States there was a fashion for antiquity, with the founding fathers depicted in artworks in white togas. In contrast, white can signal delighted exuberance, as when the British actor Peter O'Toole found fame in Hollywood: 'I woke up one morning to find I was famous. I bought a white Rolls-Royce and drove down Sunset Boulevard, wearing dark specs and a white suit, waving like the Queen Mum.'[23]

The white suits of John Travolta in *Saturday Night Fever* and Don Johnson in *Miami Vice* are images that resonate with sartorial verve. More recently, in among the pink, orange and lime sharp-cut suits worn by the stylish *sapeurs* of the Congo region, it is the white suit that stands out most splendidly, a symbol of proud defiance in the war-torn shantytowns where they live, as impressive as the opulence of a starched white linen tablecloth in an otherwise shabby dining room.

Across the Western world, women's flimsy white dresses, following the finds of Herculaneum, aped the chitons and *stolae* worn by Greek and Roman women. It was white fabric that was used for these modern-ancient styles, fluid and semi-transparent, revealing the body beneath and based on a perceived sensuality of the past. Because of this connection with antiquity, the idea has prevailed that there is something inherently sophisticated and 'classic' about the colour white. Marlene Dietrich is pictured in 1933 wearing a white trouser suit, languid with withheld sensuality; Bianca Pérez-Mora Macías, for her wedding in 1971 to Mick Jagger, wore a white YSL *Le Smoking* jacket. Such masculine-tailored styles are worn plain and simple and, whether Dietrich's trousers through a haze of Turkish cigarette smoke or Pérez-Mora Macías in jacket and tie with nothing beneath, they suggest the greater status of unadulterated male dress, a distant echo of the himation of a high-class citizen of antiquity.

TWO

The Spiritual, the Professional and the Uniform

What a strange power there is in clothing.
Isaac Bashevis Singer

White is associated with the mysterious, with the spiritual and the otherworldly. It can also suggest certain elevated values in sports clothing, in scientific and medical garb and in uniforms in general.

During the medieval period, the ghostly white-clad lady occurs in many a folktale and, for a fancy-dress party today, appearing as a ghost is an easy option since all it requires is draping a white sheet over one's head while waving one's arms about and moaning. And so it seems that white can represent the insubstantial. Angels and fairies are often depicted in ethereal white: now you see them, now you don't. White is the non-colour that seems to best express uncertainty, or at least those aspects of our experience that cannot easily be voiced, that are said to rely on faith and on what cannot be readily tested. White clothing here stands for otherness, for what is outside and beyond concrete fact.

The newborn baby is traditionally dressed in white for Christian baptism, its face emerging from a chrysalis of gauzy material, with the priest in a bright, white surplice, stiff brocade, the liturgical lace over a darker cassock beneath. It is important for the cloth around the child to seem fresh, as good as new, 'as a symbol of purity as well as

A white sheet over the head can represent a supernatural being:
Honoré Daumier, *The Phantom*, 1835, lithograph.

wholesomeness. Unsoiled fabric represents promise and responsibility.'[1]
Even the most minor introduction of colour can seem at odds with the
ritual celebration of someone's entry into the world, sullying the sense
of a new beginning, a blank slate, an unmarked whiteboard. Freed by
the sacrament from original sin, the purity of the child is symbolized
by faultless white and, like the Lamb of God, is perfectly unsullied:
'Make me white, O' Lord, and cleanse my heart; that being made white
in your Blood of the Lamb I may deserve an eternal reward.'[2]

Pastel colours and cheerful appliqués come later. In the West, at least, white fabric is considered most appropriate, the mother often choosing to wear white herself, as if in her new role she too is born again. The attention-seeking bridal display is past, replaced by the new role of maternity, of nurse and nun, clean and pure. In contra-distinction, a christening gown that has been handed down through many generations, and which may show signs of wear and careful mending, has additional value, having stood the test of time, and represents the continuation of life. Since ancient times babies have been wrapped in swaddling bands, made from white linen for those of means, swathed like a vulnerable larva, to both protect and comfort them. Some have viewed this practice as restraining the infant. In the eighteenth century, ideas about freedom of the individual led to criticism of such early constraints: 'No sooner does the infant emerge from the mother's womb, no sooner does he begin to enjoy the free-dom of movement, than we shackle him with new fetters. We wrap him in swaddling bands.'[3] However, this link between white garments and the unblemished, stainless child takes from antiquity something of the gravitas of the gods in their fair-weather cloudy realm, high in the snow-topped mountains, where white 'was sacred to Zeus, the king of the gods, white horses drew his chariot, and white animals were sacrificed to him by white-robed priests'.[4]

In the New Testament the Virgin Mary gives birth to Jesus in a stable: 'And she brought forth her firstborn son, and wrapped him in swaddling clothes, and laid him in a manger; because there was no room for them in the inn' (Luke 2:6). God made man is associated with the idea of ordinary simplicity through plain white swaddling bands. A babygrow fails to acquire quite this resonance. In the Bible, the colour of Christ's clothing is

Bride baby: handed-down christening dress, 1905–6, photograph by C. M. Bell.

31

Jesus Christ in the Temple: James Tissot, *Woe unto You, Scribes and Pharisees*, 1886–94, opaque watercolour over graphite on grey wove paper.

rarely described, though when it is, it is often said to be red, possibly referring to the seamless chiton for which soldiers are said to have cast lots at his crucifixion. It has been argued that he would not have worn white because of ancient Jewish law, since the cloth would then have required bleaching or chalking, which was considered unclean, although the Essenes, a Hebrew sect, held that it was vital to always wear white.[5] When Jesus is described as going with three apostles to a mountain to pray, he is transformed: 'And his raiment became shining, exceeding white as snow, so as no fuller on earth can white them' (Mark 9:3).

In Western art both high and low, Christ is frequently depicted in glowing white robes, suggesting that white seems most fitting to distinguish a God-made man from others. Since the Middle Ages white has been the colour of liturgical vestments for Easter and Christmas and for the festivals of saints in Roman Catholicism.[6] The religions of the world often try to communicate a sense of humility and majesty in their adoption of hard-to-maintain white vestments for their prophets.

In the ancient Indian religion of Jainism its nuns and monks wear simple white cotton robes, though its Digambara sect eschews all worldly possessions, including clothing.

White is not only worn at weddings and on festive occasions but sometimes at funerals, Zoroastrians ritually washing their white clothes after both ceremonies. Celtic Druids wear white. The ritual robes and caps of modern-day Wicca priests are white, with little or no ornamentation, symbolizing their otherworldliness. Mormons wear white for temple services and the Yoruba people weave white fabric in order to communicate with their ancestor spirits. White

Lady enticing a peacock with a strand of pearls, wearing a diaphanous pale robe, set in the Punjab hills, c. 1800, gouache and gold on paper.

clothing is sacred in Voodoo, and the robes of the new order Ku Klux Klansmen, post-1915, are floor-length and white, the faceless hood hiding everything apart from the eyes, to preserve the wearer's anonymity. Spiritual power and sometimes malevolence can thus be expressed through an enveloping white palette.

In the Book of Revelation, all in heaven are 'clothed in white raiment' (3:5), and throughout white clothing is allied to spiritual purity and heaven itself: 'And the armies which are in heaven, clothed in fine linen, white and clean, followed him on white horses' (19:4). Within the small Middle Eastern Mandaean sect, based in southern Iraq until the Iraq War, white is worn for all their ceremonies, as 'the heavenly dress of light, worn by angels and pure souls'. In baptism, a believer must 'Cover [themselves] in white like the garments of radiance and coverings of light. Put on white turbans like resplendent wreaths.'[7]

Rabbis wear white on Yom Kippur, to signify the holiest day: 'Though your sins are like scarlet, They shall be as white as snow; Though they are red like crimson, They shall be as [white] wool' (Leviticus 16:4). Orthodox Jews follow strict dress codes, as in the case of Haredi Jews, labelled by some 'Oreos' after the dark biscuit with a white centre, because of their distinctive billowing white shirts in contrast to their dark suits and hats. The white cotton tallit, or *tzitzit*, is a prayer shawl, with tassels at the four corners which are intended to remind the wearer of the laws of the Torah: 'The Lord said to Moses, "Speak to the people of Israel, and bid them to make tassels on the corners of their garments . . . to look upon and remember all the commandments of the Lord" (Numbers 15:37–41). For all Jewish festivals the scrolls and pulpit are usually covered with white cloth and white clothing is worn, following the Lord's advice to Moses, as a sign of humility and purity: 'He shall put on the holy linen coat, and shall have the linen breeches on his body, be girded with the linen girdle, and wear the linen turban; these are the holy garments' (Leviticus 16:4).

A nun's white headdress in Christian practice signifies both partial or full entry into the religious life, and also represents the quiet, feminine virtues of convent life:

Model wearing a nun's habit, fine white muslin that suggests
purity and chastity, photographic print by Fitz W. Guerin.

Mout sont sobres, blanches et netes
Et plus assez que violetes
Defuient tai, fumier et fanc.
Mout sont les chainze bel et blanc
Et bien ridé et bien lié
Soëf flairant et delié.[8]

Very modest, white and clean are they,
and more than violets

do they shrink from dirt, filth and muck.
Their linen is fair and white,
well-pleated and tied,
sweet-smelling and fine and delicate.

Fashionably dressed nuns under Hildegard of Bingen were crit-icized for the excessive beauty of their garb: 'your virgins stand in the church [in] white, silk veils, so long that they touch the floor.' Hildegard defends their appearance, as 'lucent symbols of her be-trothal to Christ': 'I saw that a white veil to cover a virgin's head was to be the proper emblem of virginity. For this veil stands for the white garment which man once had, but subsequently lost in Paradise.'[9]

It seems that whiteness is not only associated with humble dedication but represents sexual purity, the nuns' un-besmirched virginity. Christ himself was said to be born of a virgin and, as seen in medieval art, his white swaddling remains unsullied in a dusty stable, representing his mother's bodily purity.

Much of the fine work required for priestly vestments was under-taken in convents. In Saxon England, Aethelswith, an anchorite nun living on lands belonging to the Isle of Ely, devoted her time to needle-work, in particular exquisite gold embroidery for the abbot's silken copes and mitres.[10] A pure woman, in the sense of being virginal or at least leading a celibate life, was thought to be the appropriate source for spiritual clothing, and to provide a conduit between ordinary people and God.

In Muriel Spark's *The Abbess of Crewe* (1974), the eponymous Alexandra is fighting to stay in power and is acutely conscious of the effect her image has on the other dark-robed nuns. Her contrasting white habit establishes and reinforces her authority. She 'freshly chang[es] her white robes' between Matins and Lauds so that she is equally impressive throughout the day and night.[11] All the nuns wear white coifs, a cap covering the top, back and sides of the head, but in her case the coif completes her overall whiteness, and thus confirms her status – but also implies an association with death: 'Her face is a white-skinned English skull, beautiful in the frame of her white coif.'[12]

Hieronymous Wierix, after Albrecht Dürer, *The Virgin with Child in Swaddling Clothes, c.* 1580–1619, engraving.

Since early Christianity undyed white cloth, usually wool, was worn by several monastic orders and, in more opulent form and cut, by the pope himself. Comparing white with black habits for monks, Peter the Venerable speaks of 'white as the colour that in the Scriptures represents *gaudium et sollemprietas*, that is, joy and "solemnity" in the sense of festive formality: it is the colour of the radiant transfigured Christ'.[13] Pope Alexander VI expressed the wish to process through the streets of Rome in white to beseech God to allay a devastating storm, but when he was told that white vestments were traditionally worn to express joy, he opted for violet instead.[14] The Vatican displays centuries-old papal vestments that are predominantly white. They

Elaborate muslin cap, designed to be alluring: *A Man Trap*, 1780, mezzotint.

are often richly embroidered with gold and silver, worn with white watered silk soutanes and white fur-lined capes and skullcaps, as in the Francesco Podesti painting of 1854, with Pius IX surrounded by his cardinals and high officials, proclaiming the dogma of the Immaculate Conception. However, there are occasions when, in contrast, papal clothing on show is plain as can be, as with the unadorned *camiciola e calzoni*, the shirt and breeches, of Pius VII.

Female postulants wear white as would-be brides of Christ to symbolize purity. Roman Catholic vestments are white for the Virgin Mary's feast days and in Evangelicalism they represent Jesus Christ. White robes evoke the image of transfiguration.

White has come to signify the ethical, like black in its colour-free gravitas, but largely without black's potential menace. In this context, ideas about maintaining a pure and serious demeanour are outer – that is, visible to others – and often demonstrated by details of dress such as caps, aprons, cuffs, stockings, socks, gloves, ruffs, jabots and collars. White nightgowns, however, worn in the privacy of the bedroom, and underclothing that is customarily hidden from sight, are inner. Such associations are as important in religious as they are in secular garments. The inner white garment is typified by the Dominican priest's habit, for though they became known as black friars, their habit was made of white wool, with only the outer covering of a black-hooded *cappa* cloak. In contrast, the military Knights Templar wore white mantles and surcoats over their armour, the outer colour perhaps reducing the military severity of their garb as soldiers of Christ against the so-called infidel. This also emphasized, by way of its insignia, the message of the blood-red cross. Carmelites wear brown habits, suggesting they are of the earth and so practical, but conversely their cloaks are white.

In the Church of Jesus Christ of Latter-Day Saints white is worn for baptism and white shirts and ties have been adopted as male dress for temple worship – something that has become somewhat of a trend more generally for bridegrooms, not so much a symbol of purity as one of sartorial verve. The Prophet Muhammad describes those who are sinless as being 'like a polished mirror or a white cloth'.[15] Muslim pilgrims change into white clothing when they approach Mecca to symbolize a state of spiritual purity,[16] and in the Old Testament the Messiah 'is like fuller's soap', which is to say, like cleansed white wool. In Iran, post-Revolution, the all-encompassing colour for women's dress became black, with occasional forays into navy and dark grey. However, since black is closely associated with mourning and grief, paler colours are frequently worn under the outer dark manteaux or chadors. The journalist Masih Alinejad launched an online campaign, 'My Stealthy

Freedom', in 2014 in part to question the enforced hijab law. She was pictured either bare-headed or in a white scarf. There was a tide of support from women within Iran, and in 2017 Alinejad launched the White Wednesdays campaign, which encouraged the wearing of white headscarves or shawls, as a symbol of peaceful protest.[17]

In Turkey, there is much debate around *nefis*, a term that means women's vanity and envy of women, which some claim they cannot control, and that it in turn infects other women.[18] It is associated with wearing light, fancy clothing, with white being the worst offender, suggesting they are not performing their supporting, maternal roles. Among those whose dress has changed very little over the centuries are Arab men, who – even those of modest income – are commonly seen wearing spotless flowing, gauzy white robes, be they silk or cotton. In the dust of the desert, their clothing needs to be washed frequently, by women who are usually dressed more practically in black. Those women who adopt traditional dress in Egypt today but who are wealthy enough to employ servants to do their dirty work nonetheless often wear a voluminous black mantle over their fine white *yashmak*s when in public.

The officers of religion can influence the way we adorn ourselves, so that even if we do not follow this creed or that, we are often con-strained to dress modestly and with a certain formality in religious contexts. The diversity of clothing worn by imams and rabbis, monks and nuns, shamans and priests all tend to hark back to earlier times, as if their vestments represent the higher standards of the past and a superior morality. More generally, there are patterns in our everyday use of white clothing that connect with ideas about lost purity, among even the most secular.

In military uniform, for instance, where one might expect practical concerns to be uppermost, there exist some anomalies. Hannibal's Spanish infantry of antiquity wore white tunics edged with crim-son and the Cheshire archers donned green-and-white jackets in the fourteenth century, but such examples are hard to find. On the whole white uniforms were kept for formal celebrations rather than the battlefield. When white was adopted for battle, its inherent *élan*, when worn by officers who were able to maintain it, might well have

Royal Engineers, Singapore, 1878, photograph by J. E. Taylor.

emboldened them and encouraged their men to defy the enemy.
Even when smokeless gunpowder was invented in the 1880s, making
white or bright-coloured uniforms much more easily seen by enemy
snipers, many remained proved reluctant to give them up for the latest
camouflaging khaki cloth. Previously, when uniforms had begun to
be provided for conscripted men, officers were resistant to wearing
them, disliking the idea of the *griffe* of livery. They felt demeaned by
them, such measures putting them on too much of a par with their
men, because now they were all dressed more or less the same. It is
unsurprising, therefore, that many of the earliest officer uniforms
declare their greater means and status. Russian and Bavarian generals
were resplendent in fine cream wool handsomely embroidered and
adorned with large gold epaulettes and ropes and polished buttons.
Elite Russian cavalry and horse guards had white parade uniforms
made of high-quality woollen cloth, and in the summer soldiers and
officers in many regiments wore white linen shirts with their uniforms.

In the Soviet era, white uniforms were worn by the highest ranks: generals, admirals and marshals.[19] Even today there are uniforms whose apparent unsuitability is part of the point, their conspicuous impracticality deliberately reinforcing the respect and potential fear they are intended to cause.

Peter the Great, a reformer of many aspects of dress, liked to be seen as the head of his armies, as a God-like ruler. He appeared in a splendid, if impractical, short white *korzno* cape, draped across his shoulders and held in place by a precious fibula much like that of a Roman senator. He has been pictured in a long, flowing white wool cloak lined with ermine, his hat-crown and fine leather riding boots white as the Russian snow. Some seven hundred years earlier, Sviatoslav Igorevich, the Grand Prince of Kiev, though not naturally an impressive figure – being stout and bald with a wispy beard, a bushy moustache and a sidelock hanging limply on his cheek – dressed carefully for a meeting with the Byzantine emperor John I Tzimisces, donning an impeccable white shirt and breeches for the occasion, in contrast to the more conspicuous splendour of his counterpart.[20] He allowed himself one customary elaboration: a single but exquisite ruby carbuncle and pearl earring.[21] His white clothing suggested modesty and purity of purpose but the jewel expressed his true grandeur, for by such means can political ground be won.

The film *An Officer and a Gentleman* (1983, dir. Taylor Hackford) has Richard Gere wearing dazzling American Navy aviation whites when he passes out from his training. Like a great white archangel he is now able to rescue his girlfriend from her factory-worker life. In contrast, when John Travolta dances in a white suit in *Saturday Night Fever* (1977, dir. John Badham), the effect is equally exuberant but less romantic: he shines as he struts and shimmies in the dimly lit nightclub, surrounded by the other dancers in their more garish clothing. His waisted white suit is worn over a black shirt, just visible beneath his waistcoat/vest, as if reversing the more habitual uniform of the Western male businessman.

'White-collar' has become the term for the professional who does not work with their hands. For women it is acceptable to wear smart unfussy shirts or blouses but often with some colour, denoting someone who is a professional but not too much so, prepared to maintain her femininity and consequently be taken less seriously at times. In contrast the male who diverts from the norm of smart formality, like the political candidate who wears a blue shirt to address an audience of blue-collar manual workers, often raises his profile, suggesting that he understands what it means to engage in physical labour.

White clothing in Arctic regions or the whiteout of the desert are camouflage from enemy eyes, but there remain other warrior traditions where to argue for change on practical terms is to miss the point. The symbolic power of white is bound up with such anachronisms. The ancient Greek infantry soldier in his short white tunic and skirt of stiffened linen remains an image of vigour and physical beauty, yet this image was hard to maintain, its impracticality adding to this impression. The first Olympians were either unclothed or wore a loincloth, simple white cloth combining with naked power and youth. Roman practice was to crucify people naked, yet images of Christ on the cross usually portray him in a loincloth, a precursor of later medieval and Renaissance censorship and the introduction of the modesty fig leaf, but also acting as a mark of respect.

The sixteenth-century Italian crusade to cover up sexual parts and pubic hair on classical statues, and to discourage and disguise where necessary contemporary sculpture and painting, encouraged the idea that nudity invited immodesty and lust. Compared with the fig leaf, the loincloth of earlier times seems less prurient, once used to protect slaves working in the field from accident. Unlike the fig leaf, loincloths were also worn by actors, gladiators and athletes, much in the same way that sumo wrestlers wear them today, to protect the groin. The *rikishi* wrestler wears a white cotton *mawashi* loincloth for training, and the most senior ranks don the 9-metre-long (30 ft) *sekitori* white belt, which dates back to the Edo period. While wrestlers today are disqualified if their *mawashi* falls off during a bout, this rule appears to stem from the influence of prudish Western values and would never formerly have been an issue.

The idea of certain once-high-status sports being played today in vivid colours or in black can seem out of keeping. My cricketer grandfather would have found it hard to come to terms with the fluorescent

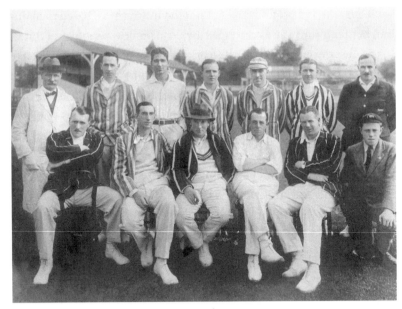

Leicester Gents Cricket team, *c.* 1921–3.

colours and contrasting commercial logos that are now worn. For him, whites represented the amateur gentleman's game. What appears to be merely a refusal to countenance change may also recognize what is lost when the simple grandeur of white clothing is cast aside.

Both polo and tennis have also had a long association with flawless white dress that is linked to certain class values. At the turn of the twentieth century women were attempting to play tennis in constricting clothing, with full-length skirts and even trains hampering their movement. *Punch* magazine suggested that men should handicap themselves when playing with women by tying their knees together. However, in pre-First World War monied society on the French Riviera, tennis had become the craze of the day. Suzanne Lenglen, known as *La Divine* (the goddess), was caught on photograph and film leaping and diving with airborne balletic grace, displaying a female athleticism that was relatively new for her time.[22] She played tennis without a corset, and on court always wore a white, barely knee-length skirt, a sleeveless top and a signature bandeau holding back her hair, its effect not unlike the criss-crossed ribbons of an ancient Greek statue. She was dressed by the couturier designer Jean

Patou, and although her interest in cutting a dash extended to brightly coloured tennis wear later in her career, it is that athletic image, all in white, that remains.

The All England Lawn Tennis and Croquet Club (AELTC) at Wimbledon had established the white-only dress rule in 1890, in an attempt to maintain the game's reputation as an elite sport. The popularity at the time of white clothing for women in general naturally extended to what was felt to be appropriate on the hallowed courts. The Queen's Club in Barons Court similarly prided itself on its exclusive membership: 'Ladies and gentlemen attired in spotless white arrived in limousines to play the elegant game.'[23] It was not so much how fast and efficient your game was, but how effortlessly you seemed to play, that was important for the image of the affluent amateur.

Later, designers such as Teddy Tinling attempted to counter the tradition of wearing white alone by introducing colourful clothing to the game, 'to bring femininity back to the court', he claimed, but Wimbledon did not agree.[24] The only adornment allowed then (and now) were narrow bands of colour at neck, hem and cuffs, on sleeve-bands and socks, and also on undergarments (that might be

Tennis party, Bombay, c. 1915.

glimpsed), all of no more than 1 centimetre (⅖ in.) wide, an echo perhaps of the scarlet and purple banding on the ancient toga and himation. One argument that persisted from the 1880s was that sweat stains were vulgar, suggesting the manual labour of the working class, and that such embarrassing marks were less visible on white fabric. As the game became gradually more athletic clothing needed to allow for greater movement, but women were still not permitted to wear shorts. Tinling had the American player Gertrude Moran obey the colour proscription, but for the Championships in 1949 wear white lace-trimmed knickers with a skirt short enough for them to be visible at times. Her public profile rocketed and the Marx Brothers, who were in London at the time, asked her to join their act. Tinling claimed later, a little disingenuously possibly, to have been most surprised:

> 'I thought a little lace trimming might look nice. It was
> nothing special. In fact it was nothing more than what my
> mother would have called kitchen lace' . . . A racehorse, an
> aircraft and a restaurant's special sauce were named after
> her. She was voted the best dressed sportswoman by the
> u.s. Fashion Academy. The whole thing was staggering.[25]

Pictures in the papers were taken from every low angle available, showing 'Gorgeous Gussie' displaying her lacy underwear. The AELTC accused her of 'bringing vulgarity and sin into tennis', and even voiced concerns about the effect on the royal family.[26] Questions were asked in Parliament. It seems that it was not enough to wear white to maintain standards of decency but that, in order to be seemly, white had to be modest and plain, or risk offending and threatening a hallowed institution.

In more recent times, as Wimbledon has remained the only major tournament to maintain the white-only rule, players have attempted to object. Andre Agassi is one of the most notable examples, refusing to play from 1988 until 1990, saying he preferred to wear the bright colours of his own branded sports clothing. Roger Federer was instructed to change his orange-soled shoes to white in 2013 and Martina Navratilova was reprimanded by the club for wearing a blue-striped skirt in 2014 because it was not up to code.[27] Institutions are sometimes said to survive on their intransigence. Tinling, for his part, in both challenging the colour code and designing the sinfully frilly knickers, was kept out of Wimbledon. It wasn't until 1982, some 33 years after the fuss about Gussie, that he was invited back to the grounds.

Although the white code has long been criticized as outmoded and sometimes snobbish, it has also tempered aspects of commercial advertising. As the game gained more general popularity, its logos and branding lent themselves to the increasingly sporty fashions of the high street for the non-athlete – trainers, T-shirts, joggers and so on. Their relative absence from Wimbledon ironically makes the London tournament appear all the more prestigious. At Wimbledon sponsorship must at least be kept low-key and stick to white.

Most of the world's sporting events where white-only was once the rule have ceded to the allure of colour. However, attire that is without indication of its provenance can seem dull, derided for being generic and as lacking individuality. The Wimbledon rule works because it maintains the kudos of being the only major tournament where white must be worn, and advertising both for the event itself and for associated items of clothing have learnt to take full advantage. Sweat-stained but Wimbledon-white apparel is balled up and flung into the crowd by victorious players, to be sold later on eBay, perhaps. An advertising campaign of 2021 for Sipsmith has an anthropomorphic swan confused as to whether it is promoting Wimbledon or gin. The bird may have his facts back to front, but Mr Swan is dressed, of course, in impeccable whites.[28]

White continues to be worn for a number of high-status sports. Some cricket tournaments have required white dress since the 1800s, to reflect heat, it was claimed, and make the red ball more visible. Such attire – initially the elegance of loose flannel bags and billowing shirt – has also become associated with the gentlemanly values that the game is sometimes said to represent. The popularity of croquet in the 1860s conjures photographic images of women in white *broderie anglaise* dresses in hazy afternoon sunshine, and in the twentieth century the white rule was also widely adopted for the leisurely game of lawn bowls. The fitted trousers and chukka shirts of the game of polo, 'the sport of kings', speak of both physical assurance and affluence. Polo players from Pakistan to Argentina favour a uniform of spotless, figure-hugging white.

Professional scientific clothing has undergone a major change of late. Once it was the starched white cap and apron of a nurse that indicated her devotion to both cleanliness and to our care. Their uniforms were initially derived from the habits of medieval nuns, suggesting a coming together of personal and institutional morality, 'their ample, loose robes of humble, often coarse fabrics are both unprovocative and a protection against the temptations of the world.'[29]

Even when all white was impractical, sleeves were protected with white linen over-sleeves and easily replaceable dickies, versions of the bib-like *guimpe* of a traditional nun's habit. The image of the Lady with the Lamp, Florence Nightingale, in her bonnet and full apron, descends from the first nursing nuns.[30] Doctors were slower to take up the idea that everyday clothing could be dangerous to their patients, wearing their tweedy civvies with little idea of the threat they represented. Gradually white coats, which could be boil-washed, were accepted as a means of preventing cross-contamination and in time became an indicator of a doctor's professional standing and respect.

However, on closer inspection Nightingale's own designs for nursing uniforms seem equally unsuitable, with long-sleeved grey wool 'wrapper' dresses and dark jackets and cloaks. All would have been difficult to wash and dry and would have disguised dirt and therefore harboured infection, despite the superficial addition of white lacy collars, caps and over-cuffs to suggest cleanliness. Her fifteen nuns, part of the small group of nurses who went with Nightingale to the Crimea, wore white wimples over their dark serge tunics. It was a style that had hardly changed from the common dress of women in medieval Europe. In this respect, nursing nuns in their starched white linen were the first to wear hygienic uniforms. The Daughters of Charity in their distinctive flying cornette headpieces were founded in the seventeenth century by St Vincent de Paul. The order was encouraged to step away from their cloistered life and attend to the poor and sick. In *The Flying Nun*, an American television sitcom of 1967, the butterfly-like linen wings are comically exaggerated, becoming more like aeroplane than celestial wings, with the winsome Sister Bertrille, played by Sally Field, able to fly to the aid of people in need thereby.

Traditional habits have experienced something of a return to popularity among young women seeking a more ordered life. The Dominican Sisters of St Cecilia, for example, claim the habit as a welcome symbol of their vocation. Sister Mara Rose McDonnell refers to her white clothing as her wedding gown and passport to happiness: 'It tells others that there's a reality beyond this world. There's heaven. We're all orienting ourselves towards heaven.'[31]

Today practical, unisex, colourful and more casual loosely styled scrubs have won the day for nurse and doctor alike. By 2007 in British hospitals the NHS did away with white coats for doctors, claiming that it would have a positive effect on the control of superbugs, their cuffs having harboured the very bacteria that they were battling. Recently this finding has been questioned, and trials are taking place to see if white coats have advantages for the patient, albeit short-sleeved to lessen the risk of infection. Whereas children are reported to feel significantly less anxious when hospitalized if they are looked after by nurses in informal and colourful clothing, adults sometimes react differently, since 'older generations may prefer white nurses' uniforms due to their association with professionalism and approachability.'[32]

Studies have shown that T-shirts and a generally less formal appearance have raised anxieties in older patients concerning competency, seriousness and cleanliness. Moreover, some say they prefer their doctors not to dress like nurses, finding the appearance of authority and status reassuring. On the practical front, colourful scrubs, unlike white fabric, cannot be boil-washed and so ironically are more likely to harbour disease. Coloured scrubs, if washed at high temperatures, lose their dye and the fibres rot.

In the field of dentistry short-sleeved white cotton tunics have long avoided the problem of dirty cuffs, though green scrubs with disposable aprons still serve for surgery. In a study concerning patients suffering from pain in the temporomandibular joints of the jawbone, all the participants were told they were to have occlusal equilibration to adjust their jaws, whereas this was only in fact done to half the group. Both groups were further subdivided into those treated by dentists wearing white coats and by those not wearing them. 'From the results of the study the largest single factor in the improvement of the jaw joint was if the operator was wearing a white coat.'[33]

A great many individuals discover a variation in their blood-pressure levels when a reading is taken in a doctor's surgery compared to when one is taken on a home monitor. 'White coat syndrome', where a patient's blood pressure is higher at the doctor's clinic than it would be if recorded at home, suggests that one can have too much respect for a doctor's status. We are reassured by the lower reading when we are less anxious at home. On the other hand, it would seem to be to our advantage for white-coat syndrome to reveal our heart's behaviour at times of stress.

During the COVID-19 pandemic, disposable coloured plastic aprons, caps, gloves and masks have been worn in contexts where in the recent past one would have expected to see white boilable cotton being used, which was at least more comfortable to wear. Do the professionals involved have any regrets about the loss of whites? Senior hospital consultants sometimes still wear white coats, and they are worn far more commonly in American hospitals. Perhaps it is the case that professional confidence is still gained from white dress, not unlike the all-white high-status value in some sports. Strangely, white coats continue to be worn by expert scientific witnesses in television adverts and online presentations, even when this would not in reality be their practice at work. A white coat, it seems, can still foster trust, particularly useful when what is being sold might otherwise seem dubious, such as treatments to restore or remove hair, or rewind one's age. Its long association with healing and hierarchies of learning can reassure us that this or that cure is born of a long line of expertise.

In the nursing profession many claim that white uniforms can be positively untherapeutic, for nervous children or drug addicts, say, fearful or distrustful of authority and of formality. But what may be of concern to the patient may be helpful for a professional's confidence, making them feel more respected and able as practitioners. In a research study in 2012 that again looked at the effect of the wearing of white coats, university students were asked to carry out various cognitive tests. Those donning white coats performed better than those who did not. However, students who were told they were wearing a doctor's coat did better than those wearing an identical garment which was referred to as a painter's coat. Even participants who were simply shown, or asked to identify, a white coat, did better in their tests than those who were not. These curious responses were attributed to 'the symbolic meaning and the physical experience of wearing' white.[34]

It might seem to follow that it was largely the students' past associations with such coats, rather than their colour, that affected their test scores and attention levels, but I would like to suggest that the two are indivisible here. The associations of experience have become inextricably entwined, so that what the researchers refer to as the basic principle of 'enclothed cognition' is relevant to our attitudes to clothing in general, and specifically in relation to white clothing. It is of additional interest here in that it appears to undermine the popular belief that uniforms have a tendency to limit a person's individual autonomy. While it could be argued that tennis players at Wimbledon are to some degree affected by their all-white dress, making them behave perhaps more gracefully or less aggressively than at other tournaments,[35] it could hardly be said that they lose their ability for individual strategic thinking because of the imposed uniform of white clothing. Michel Foucault has suggested that a uniform in this context may actually free the individual to act with greater autonomy.[36]

In the fictional world of P. G. Wodehouse's Jeeves, the manservant has very decided views on the importance of tradition in clothing, without which he knows that society itself would be threatened. Therefore, when his employer, Bertie Wooster, returns from the Riviera with a white evening jacket, he realizes that Jeeves is likely to object. He muses nervously, hoping to persuade Jeeves:

> anybody with any pretentions to being the life and soul of
> the party was accustomed to attend binges at the Casino in
> the ordinary evening wear trouserings, topped to the north
> by a white mess jacket with brass buttons . . . This mess jacket
> was very near to my heart . . . In the manner of evening
> costume, you see, Jeeves is hidebound and reactionary.

When Jeeves comes across the item while unpacking, he pretends to assume that it must be a mistake, their conversation reported by Bertie:

'I fear that you inadvertently left Cannes in the possession of a coat belonging to some other gentleman, sir?'

I switched on the steely a bit more.

'No, Jeeves,' I said in a level tone, 'the object under advisement is mine. I bought it out there.'

'You wore it, sir?'

'Every night.'

'But surely you are not proposing to wear it in England, sir?'

I saw that we had arrived at the nub.[37]

THREE

Fashionable Men,
Veils and Gloves

I t was men who led the way in dress in the Middle Ages. Little clothing from those times has survived, particularly of the lower orders and even of more affluent costume, yet illuminated manuscripts that came out of the monasteries along with the evidence of surviving stained-glass windows and records of sumptuary laws have provided an invaluable record. Margaret Scott, an authority on medieval clothing, points out that they show 'not just what people wore, but how they wanted to look in their clothing'.[1] She mentions, for instance, how in the early fifteenth century in Scotland the rural working classes were forbidden to wear dyed clothing with bag-shaped sleeves, known as houppelandes, and in 1458 they were ordered to wear 'only white or grey' (presumably undyed) cloth on working days.[2] In the *Bible moralisée* of 1220, the women's garb follows the fashion of that time, so that Bathsheba is depicted bathing in a snowy white under-shift and a married woman's white linen headdress with *gebende* chin strap, both items typical of the early thirteenth century.[3] Bathsheba is secretly observed by King David:

> It happened, late one afternoon, when David arose from his couch and was walking upon the roof of the king's house, that he saw from the roof a woman bathing; and the woman was very beautiful. (2 Samuel 11:2)

The biblical account of King David watching Bathsheba makes no mention of what she is wearing. The clothing in the illuminated manuscript is anachronistic, being medieval rather than a depiction of ancient, biblical attire, and although Bathsheba is shown as naked, the clothing that is discarded beside her is white, suggesting her innocence compared to David's lust. The many manifestations of historic clothing that reach us from across the centuries via the design departments of film and television have been transmuted into items that are more in tune with the fashions of the moment. White is often used for more affluent women's medieval clothing, and for their veils in particular. Where there is colour, it often signifies those of questionable moral character or the exotic other. The actress Elizabeth Taylor wears white in the 1952 production of Walter Scott's *Ivanhoe*, playing Rebecca, who is scorned along with her father Isaac for being Jewish, but wears a snowy veil to suggest her essential goodness; the film version of 1982 has Olivia Hussey's Rebecca in white again, but now in transparent, twinkling nylon tulle and embellished with golden coins, hinting perhaps at her father's moneylending.

In the medieval period lawyers and academics, rather than those of the very highest status, wore close-fitting skullcaps in white linen and later – in the fourteenth century – in silk.[4] For men of status and means, following new trends in dress was becoming a pleasurable pastime as well as a way of proving their worth. Many adopted the new 'crakow' shoes, sometimes referred to as *à la poulaine*, with their exaggeratedly long toes that curled up at the end. It took deep pockets to afford to wear them in wholly impractical white, cream or silvery silk satin and kid leather. Their appearance and sheer discomfort must have astonished those in practical thick leather cowhide boots. Crakows were worn first by men and later by women too, but it was men who boasted the longest toes. Armorial versions had to be de-toed in battle – that is, cut away – when knights dismounted for man-to-man fighting. Indeed, the Luzerner Schilling illuminated manuscript of 1513, which depicts the Battle of Sempach in 1386, has a towering pile of discarded toe tips in the background. Efforts were made by Edward IV of England in 1463 to restrict all 'under the state of a Lord, Esquire, Gentleman' to shoes with extensions of no more than 5 centimetres (2 in.) long, but, as with many sumptuary laws it was largely ignored and the shoes continued to be worn. An attempt to ban them entirely was made in 1465, but already a new design was all the rage, known as the duck-billed, bear's paw or cow's mouth shoe. It was popularized by Charles VIII of France, who happened to sport an extra toe, and thus the wide duck-bill was more comfortable than narrow crakows for the royal foot. The shift in fashion towards shoes of greater width and comfort is not unlike that of the bunion-inducing winklepickers and stilettos first worn in the 1950s being overtaken by more comfortable round-toed styles of the 1970s and '80s such as Earth Shoes, Birkenstocks and Uggs. Henry VIII also favoured the more generous design, and was portrayed in his characteristic wide-legged stance in white embroidered duck-bill slippers and white silk stockings.

In the later fifteenth century some of the most elaborate head-gear was worn by men, with vast curling white feathers in their caps, sometimes strung with pearls. Such affluent, fashion-aware men wore their fine white linen shirt sleeves perhaps carefully teased out from between the slits of their silk brocade and velvet sleeves, proving their worth by the lavishness of their dress. This manner of attention-seeking dress for men was virtually to disappear from the end of the eighteenth century until the modern day.

During the Middle Ages, Europe began to have access to a greater variety of fabrics, thanks to advances in loom design and improved trade routes with China, India and the Middle East in particular:

> Cotton, linen and silk garments were a speciality of the
> Middle East, with raw textiles imported there to be worked
> into remarkable clothes for the environs of Spain, Sicily or
> Syria, all regions rich in both agriculture and sericulture,
> the cultivation of silk worms.[5]

In Korea since the Goryeo dynasty (918–1392) traditional clothing for women had consisted of the many-layered, full *chima* skirt, worn high on the chest, along with the *jeogori* top, together forming the *hanbok*. They are still worn today in both South Korea and North

Korea on ceremonial occasions.[6] Those of higher status preferred to wear bright colours and sumptuous silk fabrics, whereas the *chima* of the poor was necessarily shorter, because of the need to dress more practically for work. The shorter skirts were made of cotton and coarse linen, usually of undyed white or grey cloth, commoners being forbidden to wear bright colours. In the nineteenth century the *jeogori* was worn so short that a white sash had to be added for modesty's sake, forming a silhouette not unlike the empire-line muslin dresses of the late eighteenth and nineteenth centuries in Europe.

Sometimes such simple white cotton clothing could express compassion. In a study concerning the working classes in the first half of the twentieth century, the social historian Tatsuichi Horikiri mentions a Korean friend, the wife of a colleague, who, to comfort and show respect to Horikiri after he had been falsely accused of a crime, puts on a pure white *chima jeogori*:

> It was so stunning that it took my breath away. She was a beautiful woman, but ... [it was] not ... a superficial appeal; it was rather the beauty of a dignified and majestic elegance. I found it deeply moving that she had received me in this regal attire.[7]

In the West in the early medieval period new notions of fashion could call on plentiful supplies of wool, linen and silk for those who could afford them, and it became increasingly popular to layer clothing. If rich clothing proved something about a man's position in the world, then the more clothing on show, the more impressive the evidence. New designs were increasingly developed using expensive, newly available types of fabric. In the main they were cut in simple, geometric, flat pattern shapes that did not take a particular figure into account, similar, in fact, to the dress designs of ancient Greece and Rome. However, the increasing elaborations and design details of fashionable dress met with criticism on practical grounds, as for example in relation to riding finery that allowed little movement or to a fanciful shape of sleeve so tight that it made it impossible to raise your arms. There were questions such as whether one's legs were lean and muscular enough to suit the new close-fitting jersey leggings, or whether it was in good taste for a tunic to allow occasional sighting of one's private parts. But this concern with male fashion was to survive such disapproval, right up until men's so-called renunciation of fashion.

It was important to advertise one's wealth. Alfonso v of Aragon wore a garment so lavishly encrusted with pearls that it took a team of fifteen embroiderers two weeks to sew them in place. His queen, Maria of Castile, when deserted by her husband, in contrast adopted a nun's plain habit.[8] Men's greater pride in their clothing in this period was fuelled, in Europe at least, by the stimulus of silks brought back from the Crusades: knights in glittering silver mail, their fluttering white surcoats emblazoned with the red cross of the Lamb of God, a resplendent image of fanatical vigour.

Fashions change and change about in our desire for novelty, drawing attention to different parts of the body and thereby modifying the silhouette.[9] The woman's bliaut robe, for example, which came into vogue towards the end of the twelfth century, was cut full and then drawn into the waist with lacing to emphasize the breasts. Whereas the women of Roman antiquity bound their breasts with *mamillare* bands – much as in ancient Egyptian fashion – exposing the natural contours of the body to view, medieval fashions represent the beginnings of clothing that variously disguised and accentuated different parts of the body.[10] For centuries both male and female bodies appear transformed by each new wave of fashion. Through the use of cloth, underpinnings, belts and tight, loose and more stretchy bias-cut designs, the body could be presented in the fashionable silhouette of the day. These transformations are so persuasive that it is difficult not to believe that fashionable young women of the 1920s were somehow naturally slender-hipped and flat-chested, compared with young women born perhaps twenty-odd years before them, who were largely tall and buxom. This process has been accelerated in contemporary fashion, from season to season, where a new notion can be drawn, digitally pattern-cut, fabricated and made to order and even worn, in theory, within hours.

The first evidence of white pigment being used in paintings rather than an artist relying on chalk alone comes from the thirteenth century, Cennino Cennini later describing this new, brilliant lime white in his treatise on painting.[11] In the early Renaissance, in works by Fra Angelico and later by Botticelli, there is a harking back to the styles of the antique era in their images of fine embroidered lawn and silken shirts, but these are rendered using the new attention-grabbing white, thus elevating and making divine their subject-matter. The more people encountered this new, glamorous brilliance, the more they wanted to dress themselves in like manner, to gain the same allure, but it was a luxury only available to those of means. Imagine, for instance, the outlay and upkeep required for pilgrims travelling from Venice to the Holy Land, who were advised to take with them at least three dozen linen shirts.

For the peasant classes white clothing would seldom have been an option, being reliant on expensive fabric-bleaching treatments and the availability of a plentiful supply of water to keep such garments clean. The clothing of the poor changed little from generation to generation and comprised mostly of undyed cloth. It is important to bear in mind that, since there was no knowledge of how disease was spread, whiteness can hardly have been desirable on account of its being germ-free. Yet it must have looked and therefore seemed clean to wearer and observer. There must have been something about whiteness that made people feel it had qualities of purity and of goodness, perhaps, and even that it offered some protection against infection.

Before the innovations of later centuries, whenever possible, washing would have been done in a river, making rinsing easier, perhaps after clothing had been hot-washed to remove staining if required. Even today doing washing on the banks of a riverbed, using flat stones to rub away the dirt, is common in less developed regions, as is laying clothing out to dry on grass or bushes. This image puts one in mind of Beatrix Potter's Mrs Tiggy-Winkle, singing to herself as she does the washing,

> Lily-white and Clean, oh!
> With little frills between, oh!
> Smooth and hot – red rusty spot
> Never more be seen, oh!

The drudgery of washing linen, Russia,
photograph by William Carrick, 1860–70s.

In Viking women's graves, dark glass linen smoothers have been discovered, suggesting how valued such an object must have been, representing her womanly skill at pressing clothing. Similar items have been found in ancient Welsh graves, known as slickers. In ancient Egypt doing the laundry was so honoured a task that it was carried out by men, and those who ironed used heated metal to smooth the linen and create the narrow kilt pleats. They were known as *makwag*, and were depicted at their work on painted vases. The Romans used screw-presses for maintaining the highly valued fold lines in tunics, to make them look as new again, while the Chinese traditionally used metal pans filled with hot coals, which were then passed over cloth stretched tight.

It is no wonder that with such laborious methods as were available, the idea of a weekly wash is relatively recent, and one that came in with water on tap and the washing machine. If you were fortunate enough to have many changes of clothing, then despite infrequent laundering, you might still run to a regular change of shirt and stockings, but for many this would have been a luxury. For the majority clean linen was forever out of reach. Clothing might be shaken instead and laid out in the sun to freshen and de-infest. A major washing day would have been a rare event even in well-to-do households, as clothes washing was extremely labour-intensive and disruptive. For those of great wealth, keeping clothes clean would have required a team of designated launderers with their own offices to facilitate the washing, drying and de-creasing of clothing, together taking many days.

Although there is evidence of some early soap production, lye dissolved in water was more commonly used. It was derived primarily

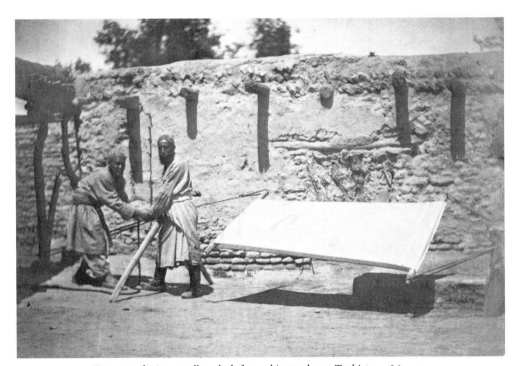

Two men drying woollen cloth for making turbans, Turkistan, 1865–72.

from urine and ash, and whitened and dislodged grease stains, though the soaking process could take many hours. It has been noted that these cleansing methods, and the slapping of clothes against stones or trampling with feet, mimic the techniques used by cloth producers, namely its weavers and finishers.[12]

There appear to have have been only minor differences in the clothing of Celt, Slav or Germanic peasant. If someone from the lower classes of society wore white, then it would have reflected well on their relative wealth and standing. Better-off peasants, whose lives were becoming less hand to mouth, could afford to wear fabrics that were difficult and more time-consuming to keep clean. Charlemagne had disapproved of such luxurious clothing even for himself and attempted in his decrees of 808 CE to inhibit this growing tendency among peasants of means.[13] Priests and monks had access to the ministrations of the convent sempstresses and laundresses for their clothing. Clerical dress may have been backward-looking in its design, but its upkeep and often expensive materials and embroidered finishes were often the finest available. Anne van Buren aptly describes a rub between those who wished to be fashionable and the clergy as 'old-fashioned clothes for the virtuous; high fashion . . . for the sinful'.[14]

In the early fifteenth century a married woman, Margery Kempe, asked Bishop Repingdon of Lincoln to allow her to take a formal vow of chastity and to don the veil, a move usually only available to widows. She reported that she had had a vision in which Christ had instructed her to wear white, so that she could become a spiritual wife and so wear 'the garments of symbolic virginity'. Although she mentioned her fear of seeming self-vaunting, since it would be bound to produce 'wonder and admiration' in others, she persisted in her ambition.[15] She compared her position to that of the Israelites in Egypt, who gained prestige from plundered gold and silver ornaments (Exodus 3:21–2). It is not clear whether she saw white as an embodiment of a God-given purpose or as a symbol of self-sacrifice, offering herself as an innocent lamb to slaughter, 'who takes away the sins of the world' (John 1:29). Her choice may never have been fully ratified, though she did wear a white habit on a visit to Rome in 1411, and in 1415 is recorded as having received communion in Norwich Cathedral in a white veil.

The anchoress, later prioress, Christina of Markyate (*c.* 1096–1155) is said to have worn the whitest of white clothing in order to protect her virginity. She is described in one of her attempts to avoid unwanted male attention as 'gathering her garments about her and clasping them close to her side, for they were white and flowing (*candidissima et subtus ampla*), passing him [the ardent Burthred] untouched'.[16] Incidentally, Christina's hagiography claims that she was an excellent needlewoman, celebrated for embroidering three white mitres for Pope Adrian vi.

One might argue that, while the clerical example encouraged a growing middle class to aspire to rich dress, the desire for and the one-upmanship of fashion as we know it was gathering force, encouraging more secular, forward-looking styles. The details of sumptuary law are beyond the reach of this book, part of the ancient history of Greece and Rome and of the Chinese and Japanese empires in particular, but it is useful here to highlight the struggle to attain the newly available glistening white cloth in the face of local and country-wide restrictions. There were many attempts to restrict people from wearing foreign materials and to encourage all but the nobility to wear what had always been worn. Since Charlemagne's decree, there had been laws curtailing the excessive consumption of luxury fabrics and fashions, mostly directed towards the laity, to control those who appeared to compete with the dress of the aristocracy. It was all very well to aspire to and copy the fashions of those in power, but for the stability of society, only the sovereign and their high officers should be seen to dress like them, to prevent sedition. Even in court circles, distinctions of status were finely tuned. For Richard iii's marriage to Anne Neville, for example, the new queen's gown was trimmed with snow-white ermine and three duchesses were given fine white cloth, but 'other countesses and ladies of lower rank had white damask to trim their gowns, with less and less being given to them as their status diminished'.[17]

Sumptuary laws were also a way of raising taxes, which in theory at least were drawn from those who could afford to pay for luxuries. The Church, holding to the fashions of the biblical past, did not, in this respect, offer a threat to the aristocracy and could be allowed their gorgeous vestments. However, there was a danger that the middle classes, in beginning to copy the clothing of their betters, might thereby think themselves as good as them, and deserving of the same privileges.

Chaucer harks back to a time before the general populace would have sought to tamper with the natural hue of God-given wool, neither bleached nor dyed:

> No madder, welde, or wood no litestere
> Ne knew; the fless was of the former hewe.[18]

> No madder, weld, or woad no dyer
> knew; The fleece was of its former hue.

The first records of levies on woollen cloth appear in 1275 in England, and sumptuary laws in London date from 1281. In the fourteenth century, Edward III attempted to promote English-made garments to preserve the social order, the flaunting of new wealth being seen as threatening political stability. Nevertheless, in 1368 Thomas Carleton was appointed as chief embroiderer to Edward, and was allowed quantities of imported foreign silks to dress the royal household. More widely, taxation made the flux of luxurious fashions all the more desirable, because they easily demonstrated monetary status. A man's *pourpoint*, the stuffed and quilted doublet jacket, for example, changed in length, fabric and elaboration right through until the seventeenth century and can be seen as evidence of how sumptuary laws failed and failed again. They may have raised revenue, but they could not stem the desire for fashionable garb.

Although monasteries may have had the means to provide their own habits and convents created the vestments required for more ceremonial dress, they would also clothe the poor and infirm with their worn-out clothing. Such a duty was ranked among the 'Seven Comfortable Works', since it was considered an act of mercy to comfort the afflicted, and could act as a penance for past sins.[19] The Council of Paris of 1212 recommended that where possible lepers should 'assume a habit', conferring on those who were often treated as outcasts 'both protection and respectability'. The clothing was intended to make them 'deserving objects of Christian compassion whose search for alms was legitimised by membership of a religious community'.[20] Dramatizations in modern times of lepers usually have them in filthy white, trailing bandages, although those who were looked after by the monasteries would have more likely been in old but clean habits, white, black and russet brown, their ulcerated limbs wrapped in strips of white cloth. However, historian Carole Rawcliffe makes the point that, despite the limited knowledge of how infections were spread, few would have wanted to wear something worn by another leper, though within the *leprosariums*, the habits and bandages must have been freely redistributed.

Both acts of mercy – such as the provision of clothing for the poor and afflicted – and sumptuary laws support the idea of dress as a visible extension of the person within. From the first loincloths, simple white dress might be said to betray the inner self, its modesty and shame. The fourteenth-century Marnhull orphrey is an embroidery of Christ on the cross. Surrounded by his tormenters, who are dressed in an array of coloured clothing, he is naked except for a silver loincloth. This loincloth is 'fetishized as a patch of pure whiteness'.[21] White is considered the appropriate colour for clothing the divine. Christ is said to have worn a seamless chiton robe at his arrest, and when depicted in art it is more often pure white, marking it apart and contributing to the soldiers' decision that it should not be divided:

> Then the soldiers, when they had crucified Jesus, took his garments, and made four parts, to every soldier a part; and also his coat: now the coat was without seam, woven from the top throughout.
>
> They said therefore among themselves, Let us not rend it, but cast lots for it, whose it shall be: that the scripture might be fulfilled, which saith, They parted my raiment among them, and for my vesture they did cast lots. (John 19:23–4)

Subsequent claims have been made that the robe survived and that parts of it now exist in a number of Christian churches, including Trier

Cathedral, and also in several Eastern Orthodox churches, where the remnants of cloth are venerated.

The Virgin Queen, Elizabeth I, in the Ditchley portrait of 1592, is a sombre figure, her face drawn, despite being arrayed in the height of sumptuous white silk excess. She found sitting for Marcus Gheeraerts the Younger tedious and it is likely that the artist would have been given access to her clothing alone to study at greater length. Elizabeth stands on a globe of the world, by implication its conquering mistress, yet even in the most flattering versions that subsequently came out of the Gheeraerts studio, she is in the last years of her long reign. Her satin dress may stand for the now familiar associations of chastity and purity, yet her age and deteriorating state of health lend the painting a touching poignancy. White is not always flattering to a fading complexion. The skirt is studded all over with a cross-banded quilt of pearls, rubies and other jewels, all set in mounts of gilded enamel. The rounded shape of her farthingale makes her skirt fall from her waist in a smooth arc, mirroring the form of the earth beneath her feet. A white triangular stomacher casts light upwards towards her face, framed in its high, ornate starched ruff, the delicate white pleats suggesting the rays of the sun itself. She is presented as a source of warmth and power, the newly fashionable wired veil like the wings of an immortal goddess. Moreover, she is strung with ropes of pearls, with a triple strand about her neck. Pearls in Greek and Roman mythology represent female beauty, of Aphrodite and Venus, and are also a symbol of Diana, the goddess of the moon. While Catholic Spain is all glittering, glimmering, shadowy black tailoring, the court of Elizabeth I is glowing, translucent white.

Beneath this splendid carapace her body is both protected and re-formed to provide the desired silhouette. Underclothing would have consisted of a white linen shift and stockings, either in bias-cut cloth or knitted and held up with garters above the knee. Elizabeth was so taken with a gift of white silk stockings in 1561 that, from that day forward, she is said to have refused to wear anything else.[22] This knitted silk was often worn over woven stockings, to protect them from her sweat. Silk had long represented the essence of luxury in cloth and yarn. Ornamented silk fabric, imported from Europe, held a sense of opulence; in a recorded case of such material from Sicily, the fabric was 'adorned with translucent gems, pearls also are either included whole in golden settings or are perforated and connected by a slender thread'.[23]

In colder weather many would have worn woollen stockings, though it is likely that they would have been cut off at the foot to prevent them from becoming grubby, since it was widely believed that wool should not be washed. Doing so might remove lanolin, which was thought to protect one against the damp and to resist dirt. This belief might well have been applied even to a monarch's laundry. Historian Joan Think investigates the progress of stocking production, from the hand-knitted to the early mechanical knitting frame invented by William Lee in 1589.[24] Handmade stockings re-mained finer in quality and there was a lack of take-up in England for the new frames. Elizabeth I denied Lee a patent, voicing con-cerns that they would put hand-knitters out of work: 'Thou aimest high, Master Lee. Consider thou what the invention could do to my poor subjects. It would assuredly bring to them ruin by depriving them of employment, thus making them beggars.'[25] Resistance to the stocking-knitting machines was such that Lee had to take his business to Rouen, which was consequently to become an even more important centre for textile production.

Elizabeth was also concerned about the effects of certain laundry products, specifically banning blue starch in 1595 to quash a craze for wearing blue-white starched ruffs, which had become associated with loose living. However, Parliament soon allowed its use again, claiming that many poor people relied on using the blue starch in order to make an honest living.[26] Similar products in various guises have hardly been absent since. More recently it has been marketed as Dolly Blue, its packaging designed to look like a mini washing dolly. Reckitt's Crown Blue is a laundry whitener originally sold in little cubes, a penny each, to disguise any hint of aged yellow in muslin and flannel. Of course, adding a hint of blue to white does not nec-essarily make it any cleaner; it just gives the appearance of doing so, which is often more to the point in our desire for visibly unblemished whites. Reckitt's Crown Blue was made from synthetic ultramarine and baking soda and became a laundry essential right up until the mid-twentieth century. Eliza Elder, laundress to the Prince of Wales, recommended the product to the public:

> I have been laundress to the Prince of Wales for several years, and I consider Reckitt's Paris Blue is the best I ever used, and is undoubtedly greatly superior to the old-fashioned thumb or dark blue. (12 April 1873)[27]

Similar products using indigo, more generally referred to as 'stone blue', had been available since the eighteenth century and were used to brighten lace collars and fine muslin. In 1775 the author Amelia Chambers, in *The Ladies Best Companion*, described the complicated processes of its use with starch to wash white linen:

> Moisten the quantity of starch you want to use, according to the quantity of your cloaths, with water, and put as much stone blue as is necessary. When the starch and blue are properly mixed, then let the whole boil together a quarter of an hour longer, taking care to keep stirring it, because that makes it much stiffer and is better for the linen. Such things as you would have most stiff, ought to be put first into the water, and you may weaken the starch by pouring a little water upon it. Starch ought to be boiled in a copper vessel, because it requires much boiling, and tin is apt to make it burn. Some people mix their starch with allom, or gum Arabic, nothing is as good as isinglass, and an ounce of it is sufficient to a quarter of a pound.[28]

Elizabeth I's ruffs would have relied upon careful maintenance. In the Ditchley portrait, to accentuate the queen's bust and taper her waist, she would have worn a pair of bodies, or whaleboned corsets, a wide farthingale, a boned petticoat and over it linen-covered padded rolls, higher in front and lower at the back, to soften the line of her skirts. Her collars, ruff and veil suggest not the pagan sun but a Christian saintly halo. To create such a ruff, a strip of white lawn or batiste up to 17 metres (55 ft) long would be intricately pleated, pressed with a goffering iron and sewn to a linen collar. Its weight would have been supported with a metal frame.[29] 'Ruff' was, incidentally, slang for a woman's genitals, so the spotless, starched linen is undercut by a sly hidden meaning at odds with the grandeur and unassailability of the ageing virgin queen.

And then there is Elizabeth I's face: that lasting blank image of authority. The carefully fashioned illusion of clear, white skin was effected by daily applications of white lead paste and vinegar. Smallpox scars and wrinkles are masked but the lead caused her hair to fall out, rotted her teeth and may well have poisoned her blood. Surrounded by her ladies in waiting, dressed in white to maintain the impression of youthfulness, she was not so much Walter Raleigh's 'lady whom time had surprised' but had become her own timeless image.

For someone of lower status, it was important not to outdo a sovereign. Even a court jester had to watch their step, for making fun of the fashion choices of their employers could be risky. And how do we recognize a queen as a queen if not by the idea we have of her in our mind's eye, formed by the image we have developed of her appearance? It was vital for Elizabeth to be at the forefront of fashion at a time when dress was increasingly important, but also to avoid risking what might make her seem ridiculous, to protect her supreme body politic, and her head.

It has been said that clothing

> without a body . . . has no reason to exist; it is merely a
> lifeless mass of fabric, a soulless hide. In short, fashion
> makes the body; the garment is a tool of bodily modification.
> The conclusion is unavoidable: there is no natural body,
> but only a cultural body.[30]

One might say, therefore, that body and garment intimately depend upon each other.

To study dress within a museum, displayed by lifeless (and sometimes headless) dummies, can seem a soulless affair. The most fragile of clothing is packed away in boxes, in layers of acid-free white tissue

See the
KNIT
Krotch

"One Smooth, Single Thickness of Cloth Throughout the Crotch"

Kenosha-Klosed-Krotch
THE CLASSIEST GARMENT MADE

READ THE FOLLOWING PAGE

Male jersey underwear, both practical
and comfortable, 1916.

paper, which distance them from their former contexts and from those who may wish to view them. Yet a piece of clothing we know belonged to a relative, say, can seem to come alive. I have a few items from my own family, none of them at all exceptional. A coarse white cotton chemise of my grandmother's, with her initials in fraying red at the hem, together with a pair of my grandfather's fine-knit wool and silk long johns with pearl buttoned fly and hand-worked buttonholes, survive as objects of value partly on account of their once having been worn. They seem to resonate with their past ownership.

We may hope to draw nearer to a historical figure through a close study of what they chose to wear, how restricted they were, how dull or excessive their fabric and furbelows:

white silken laces
That ancient kings about their forehead wore.
Sweet bands, take heed lest you ungently bind,
Or with your strictness make too deep a print.[31]

So much of this is of course the imagination at work. If it were proved beyond doubt that my grandmother's chemise had never belonged to her, but instead to the Tsarina Feodorovna, Empress of Russia, or that those underpants were in fact worn by Neville Chamberlain and confused with my grandfather's at a laundry, what should I make of it? Part of the interest in television programmes such as the *Antiques Roadshow* is not only the 'unpacking' of the items brought along for valuation, but the reactions of the owners when they find out that their previous understanding as to provenance was mistaken. On occasion they may even be disappointed to discover that an item – though of considerably greater financial value than they had thought – turns out to be, let us say, a reticule netted by Rose Bertin for Marie Antoinette, and not their great aunt's snood tucked away in recent times at the back of a sock drawer and kept through thick and thin.

Was Elizabeth I constrained by others to maintain a certain display, or was she in such a position of power and influence that her fashion choices could be her own? We cannot help but be influenced by the fashions of the time, even if we might consider ourselves to have no interest in what we wear, for few are willing to step away from the shadow of what seems appropriate, be unconcerned whether an item is outdated or too avant-garde. Elizabeth was an enthusiastic follower of French and Spanish trends and wears the whalebone stays and corsets of her era, making her the epitome of high fashion and protected by its armour. Her fashionableness promotes an image that secures her crown, forcing others to follow her lead. In the refined manners of the court, the striding, posing, aristocratic male might well have felt unable to imagine dressing without a shoulder-enhancing velvet doublet with its reassuring padded peascod belly. It would have been difficult to feel sufficiently masculine without a prominent codpiece. For Elizabeth her garments become part of her belief in her God-given authority and her will to power.

Referring specifically to the end of the Middle Ages, historian Denis Bruna mentions the degree to which the body beneath was transformed, claiming, 'more than at any time before then . . . one can measure the extent to which the clothing envelops, disguises, and masks the body.'[32] That is something many of us aspire to in our clothing choices: to improve the natural and disguise the embarrassingly unacceptable.

A fashionable man about court might have chosen to express his self-confidence through excess while disdaining practicality. Robert Dudley, Earl of Leicester, when visiting Warwick in 1564, took full advantage of the prestige that white clothing begets, cutting a fine extravagant figure:

> apparelled all in white, his shoes of velvet, his stocks of hose knit silk, his upper stoks of white velvet lined with cloth of silver, his Dow[b]let of silver, his jerkin white velvet [drawn] with silver, beautified with gold and precious stones, his girdle and skabard white velvet, his Roobe white Satten embowdered with Gold a foor broade very curiously, his cap black velvet with a white fether . . . a sight worthie the beholding.[33]

During the early modern period and up until the sixteenth century, women, whatever their means, were generally less luxuriously apparelled than men. Men's and women's clothing had usually followed the same trends but, as with birds, it was the male whose glorious plumage was the more splendid. All but young, unmarried women would have kept their hair hidden from view behind a sometimes transparently fine veil of wool or linen. In Renaissance Italy this would have been the rule for all married women, and whether transparent or opaque, it was customarily in plain white, representing feminine grace. Cotton was beginning to be more readily available in the seventeenth century, garnered from India and Ceylon, but though it became more affordable it could not match the light-catching qualities of linen. Moreover, whereas cotton might look clean and fresh all day long, to see someone in impeccable starched linen was to recognize immediately that they had the wherewithal to change their headdress more regularly. In

German-speaking regions, women wore a variety of headdresses depending on where they came from, from densely padded and multi-layered fine linen to the heavily starched wings of various designs still worn by some religious orders today. Peasant women in Europe and across Russia would often have worn a simple kerchief of coarse white linen, smoothed flat across the forehead and then twisted under the chin, the tails of cloth tied at the back much as hijab scarves are worn. Northern European caps of the late sixteenth and seventeenth centuries are some of the most beautiful, true to the shape of the head, and with the stiffened linen allowing intricate multiple cuffs. They might also be padded to make the face seem heart-shaped or have a curve of starched cloth following the dip of forehead and cheek, their simple lines in tune perhaps with the non-conformist, Lutheran influence of their time. They are fine in both design and the excellence of their needlework, but ostensibly intended to demonstrate modesty and a lack of personal vanity. In contrast Elizabeth I wears embroidered linen caps and starched headdresses originating from Paris and Florence, and the evident intention is to impress.

Much the same can be said of women's collars and ruffs, sometimes eschewed altogether in Denmark where the medieval hooded shoulder cape was still being worn. Even lace ruffs, worn by the more affluent, were seldom ornamented with embroidery or jewels. However, in the 1580s ruffs became so large that they were referred to as *Duttenkragen* (cartwheels) in Germany and Flanders. In general, across Europe fine linen accoutrements are less exaggerated in rural regions, even among the well-to-do. Danish clergy today retain the plain linen piped ruff but, as with much religious clothing, it has become impervious to the flux of fashion, as set as the heavily starched collars of Catholic and Anglican clergy.

The contemporary artist Annet Couwenberg draws on her Dutch origins to investigate the meaning of lace. She makes ruff and lace petticoat forms from paper doilies and corsets from folded paper, thus representing high-value antique clothing with cheap throwaway paper, drawing attention to the contradiction that is often present in white dress. Her work is a deliberate reference to seventeenth-century portraiture, and she claims that clothing can be 'a metaphor that examines the precarious balance between the constraints of social norm and our private desires'.[34] For her the reference is personal, the doilies reminding her of her grandmother's 'desire for gentility and . . . love of ornamentation', along with being a comment on 'elite culture, readily available and easily discarded. As a commodified token of class, [the paper lace] glorifies elegance, however false'.[35]

In Shakespeare there are references to white dress and its symbolic qualities. The playwright's father was a whittawer by trade, tanning hide into leather and making gloves, and he was once found guilty of illegally trading in wool. Perhaps it is no wonder that his son was sometimes interested in what his characters wore as a key to understanding their inner life. In *Hamlet* it is Polonius, advising his son Laertes before he travels abroad, who specifically expresses a link between character and outer appearance and warns against fashionable excess:

> Costly thy habit as thy purse can buy,
> But not express'd in fancy; rich, not gaudy:
> For the apparel oft proclaims the man. (1.3)

Therefore, clothing should be of high quality but understated and never flashy, though this view is tempered by what we come to know of Polonius's character, his views often long-winded and over-cautious, and his being prepared to be underhand, making use of his daughter Ophelia to discover Hamlet's state of mind.

Bianca's name in *The Taming of the Shrew* suggests that she is blemish-free, supposedly chaste and virtuous, and consequently productions usually dress her in white. Ophelia is also often portrayed in white clothing, or in silver, as in John Everett Millais' painting of her death, in order to portray her innocence. In *The Winter's Tale* white acts as a complex metaphor to express the tortured jealousy of Leontes, who convinces himself that his friend Polixenes and his wife have sullied 'The purity and whiteness of my sheets' (1.2). In the play white implies beauty, faithfulness, old age, religious dignity and even solemnity. In *Conte d'Hiver* (*A Winter's Tale*) of 1992, one of his *Four Seasons* quartet of films, Éric Rohmer cites the scene in

Edward Fisher, after Johan Joseph Zoffany, 'Miss Farren in the
Character of Hermione' (in *The Winter's Tale*), 1781, mezzotint.

Shakespeare's play where Hermione's statue, 'So fill'd and so becoming;
in pure white robes,/ Like very sanctity' (III.3), comes back to life.[36]
In a production of *The Winter's Tale* at Stratford-upon-Avon in 1969,
my first glimpse of theatre, the set and costumes were predominantly
white. It was white on white, as if the whole world was in accord, all
except Leontes. He was dressed in white,[37] but his furiously jealous
state of mind reverberated against the calm setting of gentle wife and
kind friend. Cool white against white-hot passion.

Women's hands can represent beauty and constancy as, for example, in *As You Like It*, when Orlando swears his love 'by the white hand of Rosalind' (III.2).[38] This association extends to their gloves, which both encase and can be seen as representing the hand. A glove is entered by the hand, and so suggests both male and female sexual roles. In *Love's Labour's Lost*, tricked into revealing his feelings, Biron swears that he will no longer use poetical images in pursuit of love, but instead adopt the women's example, by using only literal language:

> I do forswear them: and I here protest,
> By this white glove, – how white the hand,
> God knows! (v.2)

Yet it is the sight of Rosaline's gloved hand and all it suggests to him that provides the highly charged symbol on which he pledges his future unpoetical straightforwardness.

Portraits during the Tudor and Elizabethan periods often include white kid gloves, jewelled and perhaps fur-lined, intimating pubic hair. Elizabeth I owned many pairs of finely tooled close-fitting gloves, and frequently gave them as presents, playing on their suggestiveness as a formal but discreetly intimate gift. Sometimes they are worn attached at the waist as a luxurious accessory of high fashion, for, when they are not worn on the hand, they can stand for bodily restraint, a suggestion of the erotic that is withheld, as was Elizabeth herself.

In the Armada portrait of 1588, the single large pearl that hangs from a white satin ribbon at Elizabeth's girdle symbolizes her chastity and dedication to her people. Although there is no contemporary evidence of what she actually wore at Tilbury, later accounts suggest she dressed in silver armour, and even a helmet festooned with extravagant white feathers.[39] The author Carolly Erickson elaborates, describing her riding out on a huge white horse:

> armed like a queen out of antique mythology in a silver cuirass
> and silver truncheon. Her gown was white velvet, and there
> were plumes in her hair like those that waved from the helmets
> of the mounted soldiers.[40]

Nicolaes Eliasz Pickenoy, *Johanna le Maire*,
c. 1622–9, oil on panel. She is depicted with an elaborate
goffered collar and holding embroidered white kid gloves.

The Ritz and Four Seasons hotels, and the smartest apartments of, say, Fifth Avenue, are traditionally known as 'white glove buildings'. Their uniformed doormen wear pristine white cotton gloves, sometimes in an honorary role, attached to one shoulder. Lately disposable latex gloves have become more widely worn, hygiene winning out over elegance during a pandemic. The doormen – for they are rarely female – may not belong to a privileged class themselves, but they 'lead an ornamental, as distinct from an industrial existence'.[41] Maids in households wishing to maintain traditional class distinctions are also sometimes required to wear white gloves, as if keeping an appropriate distance from those they serve is represented by that symbolic barrier, as well as protecting their employers from the intimacy of their employees' sweat. As the American practice of holding a prom at the end of school has spread across the more affluent world, young women wearing formal white gloves with their fancy, flouncy dresses, sometimes long to the elbow, have become a more familiar sight. Even young men can be seen sporting wrist-length white gloves, an echo of turn-of-the-nineteenth-century elegance, when it would have been considered ill-bred for a man's hand to come in contact with the naked flesh of his partner. Should you ask to examine an ancient manuscript in a library or study a fragile garment in a museum, then you are required to don white cotton gloves. Increasingly these are being replaced by lurid rubbery jobs, which apparently do still less damage, though they are certainly less pleasant to wear. Yet even a pair of ill-fitting, dusted purple latex gloves somehow retains the idea of white-gloved care. Take a Japanese taxicab: the driver is likely to be wearing slightly too large but spotless white cotton gloves, buttoned smartly at the wrist, a sign of respect for his official role rather than of subservience.

In England well-connected girls between the ages of sixteen and eighteen once faced the March to October social season, during which they were presented at court. Attending a whirl of parties and sporting events, they were supposed to set about finding suitable husbands. The practice had begun in Elizabeth I's court as an occasion for only a small, select group of the nobility. Gradually the gentry, and then the merely well-to-do and even foreigners of sufficient means, were included. By the late 1950s hundreds of young women were involved. Queen Charlotte's Ball, founded by George III to celebrate his wife's birthday in 1780, had become the major event in the debutantes' calendar. All had to wear white ballgowns with long white gloves. According to the biographer Fiona McCarthy, who took part in the last official season in 1958, the girls were schooled to descend a wide staircase into the Great Room at Grosvenor House in groups of about 150, Queen Charlotte's candle-lit birthday cake carried to the fore. She recalls the dramatic scene: 'like the maidens in a Burne-Jones painting . . . trundling in a huge white cake to the March from Handel's Judas Maccabeus . . . a massed curtsey was performed by the serried ranks.'[42]

McCarthy mentions a commentator as describing the ball as being a 'mixture of the Nuremberg Rallies and the Dance of the Fairies in the Hall of the Mountain King'.[43] White dresses alone were possibly not enough to create an atmosphere of charm and innocence, not with four hundred young women of varying degrees of attractiveness and influence, with only the prettiest being given the few starring roles at the head of this descent of the virgins.

In the Southern United States an older generation of white women still don white gloves to signify their leisured, ladylike lifestyles.[44] If such a southern belle threatens to take off her gloves, it is said to be a sign of her being about to say something of interest, like a boxer removing his gloves to cause maximum damage. The lady's maid may wear white gloves along with a cap and apron, but the significance of this outfit is somewhat different again, with white representing the required distance to be maintained. The novel *Little Women* has the two older March girls discussing the importance of wearing clean white gloves:

'Mine are spoilt with lemonade, and I can't get new ones, so I shall have to go without,' said Jo, who never troubled herself much about dress.

'You must have gloves, or I won't go,' cried Meg decidedly. 'Gloves are more important than anything else. I should be so mortified if you didn't have them . . . Can't you make them do?'

'I can hold them crumpled up in my hand, so no-one will know how stained they are; that's all I can do. No, I'll tell you how we can manage – each wear one good one and carry a bad one; don't you see?'[45]

There are many reasons for wearing white gloves, but it is important for them to be spotless, or they lose their power. As with so many items of white dress, they are not intended as a casual feature, whether the choice is the wearer's or imposed on them by another. Just as the medieval and Renaissance man relied for his sense of style and significance on a fine linen shirt and spotless stockings, white gloves are apparently minor articles of clothing that quietly pack a punch.

FOUR

Powdered Wigs and Muslins

A woman can never be too fine while she is all in white.
Edmund Bertram to Fanny Price in Jane Austen's
Mansfield Park (1814)

What happens when attention to dress is taken to extremes? When the fantastical captures the imagination of the public and press, should a minority trend be allowed to govern our view of the fashions of a period? What is considered exaggeratedly daring can of course quickly become mainstream, the reverse of this process also being commonplace, though it tends to be slower by far. Sociologist Thorstein Veblen describes the transformation of an item from high-fashion novelty to the outmoded, and then ridiculous anachronism, as exciting 'aesthetic nausea', and this analysis, he suggests, is also relevant to more subtle changes in what is considered fashionable.[1] Such an effect might be usefully traced in microcosm in relation to the rise and fall in popularity of the eighteenth-century white powdered wig. This Rococo extravagance was adopted across affluent society, influenced by the French court. The tallest, most toppling, more outrageous examples would have been rare, worn only on the most formal of occasions by the nobility, those of the highest status and income, who were able to afford the considerable assistance that such creations required. At the end of the seventeenth century it was men who took to powdered wigs. The wig was later adopted by

Variety of men's wigs, 1773, etching by Matthew Darly.

women, who, even in the first throes of the craze, preferred to use their own hair around the face, adding hairpieces and exotic appendages to extend and give extra height.

Louis xv of France was responsible for calling an end to the more extravagant examples of men's wigs. However, he permitted women to continue to wear them – a first step, it might be argued, in men moving away from the central sartorial ground, and allowing the most frivolous and sumptuous examples of fashionable dress to be worn largely by their dependent women. In time the only men wearing powdered white wigs outside the courtroom and parliament were either servants or ageing eccentrics.

When Flaubert's Emma Bovary, driven by a longing for a more romantic life, attends the ball thrown by the Marquis d'Andervilliers, she is astonished by the glamorous luxury of the evening. At dinner even the butler can delight her in his elegant clothing of 'silk stockings, knee breeches, white cravat and frilled shirt, solemn as a judge'.[2] She is thrilled by the way some women failed to put their gloves inside their glasses to stop them from being filled, as was the custom, because they were intending to drink champagne, just like the men. The evening gloves would have been of fine glacé kid leather, like a second skin, a visible but intimate article of sumptuous dress. During the quadrilles she observes the other female guests: 'scent-bottles were tilting in unclasped hands with white gloves that revealed the shape of the fingernails and marked the skin at the wrist.'[3] The whole episode lingers in Emma's sensual memory, standing in contrast to her mundane life ever after.

The dresses, the fabric, the skin, the food and the plates that bear the food, and even the very furniture all combine in her imagination as part of this drowsy, erotic world, where distinctions between skin and material seem to fade away. Here she discovers the types of men of which she has only dreamt:

> Their coats looked better cut, of smoother cloth . . . They had the complexion that comes with money, the clear complexion that looks well against the whiteness of porcelain, the lustre of satin, the bloom on expensive furniture, and is best preserved by a moderate diet of exquisite foodstuffs. Their necks turned gracefully in their low cravats; their long whiskers flowed down over their collars; they wiped their lips on handkerchiefs embroidered with large initials, and deliciously scented.[4]

When later in the novel Emma turns up at a masked ball in Rouen, she has become dissatisfied with her lover Léon and with how far she has fallen from grace. She is dressed in 'velvet breeches and red stockings, [and] a gentleman's wig'. The small, powdered wig has gone beyond the ridiculous stage of fashion that Veblen traces, suggesting a parody of the romantic ideal, in a tawdry setting and with crude companions. At first, she 'jumped about all night' for them but, taking stock in the early morning, she feels suddenly ashamed of keeping such company. Emma is in fancy dress, cross-dressed as a point of ambivalent style and wearing a club wig. How she and those she is with are dressed is in humiliating contrast to that of the elegant men she remembers from years before, making a mockery of her nostalgia for the ball at Vaubyessard. Rather than achieving the status and grace that she imagined her clothing might have brought about, instead it marks the beginning of her disillusionment and her descent into despair.

White perukes and periwigs continue to be worn in court today in the UK by judges and barristers, despite the many attempts to deride their use, seen as early as in Hogarth's *The Bench* of 1758 where four bewigged judges sit while a case is heard before them, three of them fast asleep or drunk, the other inattentive. As recently as 1992, Lord Chief Justice Taylor suggested abolishing the wearing of wigs altogether, but the argument was won by those who considered that, along with gowns and robes, they were an important aspect of traditional dress and should be kept.[5] Somehow the court wig, hot and uncomfortable to wear, potentially intimidating or simply foolish looking, has managed to survive ridicule and become a non-fashion symbol of learning and professionalism. It may not grant anonymity but, much like the masks worn during the COVID-19 pandemic, it creates a sense of interpersonal distance, and it is argued that it helps establish the would-be impartiality of the court. The barrister's wig has moreover come to grant the wearer a status denied to the solicitor. However, in the Supreme Court, a higher sphere of the law, barristers are permitted

Staff at the British Medical School, Hammersmith, 1946.
The consultants do not wear white coats.

to leave off their wigs, much as medical consultants distinguish themselves from their more junior colleagues by not wearing white coats and prefer the apparently more modest title of 'Mr' rather than 'Doctor'. So it goes on, as high-kudos clothing becomes too widely worn, necessitating a reversion to other means of distinguishing a minority that wishes to be marked out as superior.

The intricate styles of the eighteenth-century wig could turn a smoker's acrid yellow from use of the curling iron, so that when in 1726 Humphrey Ravenscroft found a way of permanently fixing curls in place, his wig makers in Lincoln's Inn London flourished. Human hair was prohibitively expensive, and it was difficult to successfully bleach black hair imported from the East. Rumours circulated that the French guillotine had provided an excellent new and cut-price source of white hair during the Terror, from such as Marie Antoinette herself, whose hair was said to have turned white from fright. White hair could either be used in its natural state or dyed other colours more successfully. Wigs were also fashioned from bleached horsehair, goat hair, fox tails, mohair, worsted and sometimes even fine wire.[6]

What would Louis XIV have been without his spectacular curls? – though it was only in his later years that he began to powder them. Around 1655, the Sun King's wish to disguise his thinning hair led to a fashion throughout the French court for the adoption of wigs, with more than two hundred *perruquiers*, that is, wig makers and dressers, said to be on call at Versailles. His cousin Charles II of England also adopted the wig, perhaps on account of his hair having turned grey from the age of seventeen, though unsurprisingly those he chose were dark and lustrous. Wigs offered a solution to men after centuries of premature balding caused by venereal disease, the lingering effects of lead poisoning and the plague. A wig could cover up patchy hair or disfiguring sores. The fact that they were known to be expensive to produce meant that a fine luxuriant wig marked the wearer as successful as well as stylish, hence the term 'bigwig'. Moreover, an apparently strong hairline without evidence of receding was even then considered the mark of a handsome, well-bred and reliable man.

Men were less likely to be accused of immodesty than women. While the lack of hair by tonsure, the practice of shaving the crown

Caricature of the fashion for tall wigs, tying the tallest to a scaffold, with perhaps a reference to the guillotine, c. 1788, etching by M. Rapine.

of the head, for example, is meant to represent religious humility, one might argue that it also suggests a lack of worldly power. No wonder then that Louis the Pious, son of Charlemagne, or Louis the Debonair as he was sometimes known, forced male relatives he suspected of harbouring ambitions against his rule to be tonsured and safely secured in remote monasteries.[7]

A powdered wig, even if old-fashioned and perhaps shabby, could nonetheless add gravitas. Four successive American presidents wore them: John Adams, Thomas Jefferson, James Madison and James Monroe.[8] George Washington did not wear a wig, preferring to powder his own hair white. Tall wigs and towering women's hairstyles became sufficiently *à la mode* in Paris for legislation to be introduced to heighten standard doorways to create easy passage for the vast, teased up-dos for those of means. There were many exotic manifestations such as sailing galleons or birds in flight. Fashions in powdered rococo hairdos were particularly fast changing, their expense coupled with their discomfort adding to their desirability. In a painting by Thomas Gainsborough of circa 1781, Queen Charlotte of Great Britain and Ireland is depicted in a gold-spangled white silk dress, the meaning of her *pouf au sentiment* hairstyle lost in time. Others were more celebrated, commemorating the Montgolfier balloon trials, for example, or representing more abstract concepts, one such seeming particularly apt, given the weight of such headpieces – *des Migraines*, or a God-awful headache.

The diarist Mary Frampton describes these high hairdos and the complexity of their construction, and the resulting discomfort of the wearer:

> At that time [1780] everybody wore powder and pomatum;
> a large triangular thing called a cushion, to which the hair
> was frizzed up with three or four enormous curls on each
> side; the higher the pyramid of hair, gauze, feathers, and other
> ornaments was carried the more fashionable it was thought,
> and such was the labour employed to rear the fabric that
> night-caps were made in proportion to it and covered over the
> hair, immensely long black pins, double and single, powder,
> pomatum and all ready for the next day. I think I remember
> hearing that twenty-four large pins were by no means an
> unusual number to go to bed with on your head.[9]

It was an extreme of fashion that was often worn only for special occasions. The business of securely attaching a wig was such a feat of engineering, and involved such expense, that women often did not like to remove them for days and even weeks afterwards, to get their full money's worth. They must have made for an awkward night's sleep. To keep the hair looking smart over its framework or toques of wool, hemp, hair and/or wire, it had to be re-powdered with a bellows, the wearer covering their face with a cone-shaped mask to refresh the desired effect. The fashion could even be themed to promote a cause, such as the renowned inoculation coiffure that Marie Antoinette wore to publicize her success in getting Louis vaccinated against smallpox.

In 1665 Samuel Pepys in London had discussed his new periwig with characteristic practical caution:

> put on . . . my new periwig, bought a good while since, but darst not wear it because the plague was in Westminster when I bought it, And it is a wonder what will be the fashion after the plague is done as to periwigs, for nobody will dare buy any haire for fear of the infection, that it had been cut off the heads of people dead of the plague![10]

At a time when there was no lasting treatment to deter infestation, a wig could at least be sent out to be deloused and re-dressed. However, towards the end of the eighteenth century, by which time powdered wigs had been worn for decades, the younger generation, particularly those blessed with a good head of hair, eschewed wigs altogether and took to powdering their own hair, and soon after to leaving it short and shockingly natural in appearance. One of the spurious criticisms that had circulated of Marie Antoinette was that she powdered her hair with flour at a time when the poor were starving, as if she were flaunting an arrogant indifference to their plight. In fact, bread flour would have been too coarsely grained, with those who could afford it preferring to use finely milled and sieved starch. Her mother, Queen Maria Theresa of Austria-Hungary, was concerned about the rumours circulating of her daughter's profligacy, advising caution in a letter of 1775 (shades of both Lord Chesterfield's advice to his son and Shakespeare's Polonius here):

> I cannot help but touch upon a point that many of the papers repeat to me too often: it is the hairstyle that you wear. They say that from the roots it measures 36 pouces [inches] high and with all the feathers and ribbons that hold all of that up! You know that I have always been of the opinion that one should follow fashion moderately, but never carry it to excess. A pretty young queen full of charms has no need of all these follies. Quite the contrary. A simple hairstyle suits her better and is more appropriate for a queen. She must set

the tone, and everyone will hurry to follow even your
smallest errors.

But her daughter makes light of such moderation, and we may shudder
at her breezy confidence, given what was to come: 'It is true that I
am a bit occupied by my hairstyle, and as for the feathers, everyone
wears them, and it would look extraordinarily out of place not to.'[11]

Washington's successors did not see themselves as men of fashion,
but as demonstrating traditional, white-haired wisdom. Pale grey,
rather than white, powder came into vogue for both genders, with
women also wearing sugared-almond colours – rose pink, lilac and
forget-me-not – and, by the end of the century, following men's fashion
by leaving their hair unpowdered.

While it is widely held that white hair is an indicator of ageing,
and women and men throughout the ages have often tried to slow its
progress, the business of applying white or pale powder to one's hair
appears to run counter to this attitude. The young have little interest
in such concerns. However, nowadays an older woman may be slow
to surrender the locks of her heyday and, as greying hair turns to
pure white, many take to the bottle. Some have a complexion that
is flattered by the impact of white hair and it may remain thick and
glossy despite its whiteness. Others are not so lucky. Some women,
such as the oldest working supermodel Daphne Selfe (born 1928), have
looks and presence that give them the confidence to carry off their
white locks; others may find the pressure to look young beyond the
pale. Oscar Wilde captures this desire to reverse the natural process
in *The Importance of Being Earnest*:

> Lady Bracknell: I was obliged to call on dear Lady Harbury.
> I hadn't been there since her poor husband's death. I never saw
> a woman so altered; she looks quite twenty years younger . . .
> [she] seems to me to be living entirely for pleasure now.
> Algernon: I hear her hair has turned quite gold from grief.[12]

In chemist shops across the Western world there are many options
for white and pale pastel bleaches and semi-permanent dyes intended

Yvonne De Carlo as Lily Munster, with her splendid particoloured tresses, in the sitcom *The Munsters* (1964–6).

for the younger head of hair. In punk and goth fashion blue-black dyed hair sometimes has a thick streak of white towards the front, much as Yvonne De Carlo wore in the television sitcom *The Munsters* from 1964 to 1966 and in the film *The Munsters' Revenge* in 1981. She played the original vampire mother, Lily Munster, and her clothes, though initially seen in a pre-colour television era, are without doubt either black or white or particoloured, no footling use of colour suitable for a gothic diva. More recently, Catherine O'Hara donned an almost entirely black-and-white wardrobe to play Moira Rose in *Schitt's Creek*, the Canadian sitcom produced from 2015 until 2020. The eccentrically fashionable actress she plays permits only a very occasional hint of colour in her arsenal of wigs.

In Japan, while some young women may be tempted to bleach their hair, doing so is rare and there seems to be little evidence of older women choosing to go pale. I was informed in Japan that this was because Japanese hair never, or hardly ever, turns white, though the quantities of black hair dye on sale at every corner kiosk would seem at odds with this view. Japanese 'white lace punk' of the late 1980s was too clean-looking and ethereal to qualify as true punk fashion, yet did sometimes involve bleaching the hair platinum blonde, which was by far the most daring aspect of the craze. The sumptuous thickness and health of much Japanese hair is highly prized, so to bleach it, damaging its condition and risking turning it an unwanted metallic hue, comes closest to the tenets of rebellion dear to UK punk of the 1970s.

The effect of Enlightenment thinking on how people wanted to be seen encouraged the appearance of natural-looking hair, even if it was then discreetly augmented by hair pieces and dye. Those who continued to wear white powder may have seemed hopelessly behind the times, although gradually powdered wigs took on their own non-fashion kudos, evidence of influence and worldly respect or, as in Emma Bovary's case, worn as symbols of past elegance, now lost.

It is difficult to envisage fashion preceding the French Revolution independently of that seismic event. We tend to account for changes in dress by looking back rather than forward, for obvious reasons. All we can safely say, with wavering confidence, is that matters are likely to change. Predictions are unreliable, and yet the fashion section in the library where I work is dominated by books on 'future fashion'. Fashion, for all its fascinations, cannot be *essential* to political change, but the reverse would seem to be true, in that fashion is influenced by its context and thus should help us to understand past events. As Madeleine Delpierre, working in the fashion department of the Musée Carnavalet in 1947, put it: 'The essence of fashion is its mutability. Without the caprices of fashion, clothing would never change, remaining as static as traditional costume.'[13]

Marie Antoinette seems by all accounts to have been taken with such caprice. She was an enthusiastic patron of the Marchande de modes, an organizing body of women's fashion merchants, in her search for the newest and most luxurious fripperies, which were often brought to her attention by Rose Bertin, a former milliner. This love of novelty, together with the influence of Rousseau's ideas, led to the queen and her ladies dressing up as shepherdesses and milkmaids in the grounds of the Petit Trianon chateau at Versailles. They wore simple white cotton muslin, with satin bows on their crooks, just like Little Bo Peeps. During her lifetime Marie Antoinette was lampooned for this mode of play-acting in dress that at first appeared to be simply made, though in its fine detail was as unlike that of a real shepherdess or milkmaid as her experience of their day-to-day lives. Her portrait by Élisabeth Louise Vigée Le Brun in 1783 shows the queen in a loose high-waisted white muslin multi-layered dress with a soft ruffled neckline and delicate puff sleeves, without jewellery, wearing a plain straw hat and holding a rose.[14] Despite claims that she was dressed indecently for one of her nobility – as if in her underclothes, it was

Marie Antoinette in white muslin and a shepherdess bonnet over her
cap, 1784, engraving by Nicolas Dupin, after Pierre Thomas Le Clerc.

said – she sent presents of what became known as her *chemises à la
reine* to her friends, including Georgiana, Duchess of Devonshire.[15]
Not only did the new cotton dresses worn by those who were able to
buy silk and velvet become popular throughout Europe, but in France,
itself in flux, it became patriotic to wear muslin, coarser cotton and
even wool. More luxurious fabrics increasingly seemed out of keeping
with the ideals of the Revolution. One might say that, in this respect,
Marie Antoinette was not only ahead of fashion but embraced the

new political climate in her fancy for plain, less expensive-looking white cotton clothing.

However, Caroline Weber argues that since India was unable to cope with the increased demand for cotton, the influence of Marie Antoinette's pastoral idyll was to lead to greater slave labour in the colonies. It has been suggested that the French queen's attempt to play at the simple, rural life, because of her ability to influence fashion, is responsible for the evils of the plantations in the newly independent United States of America, a result that in fairness she could hardly have foreseen.[16]

As political dissent grew, the wearing of an all-white cockade, pinned to a shirt front or nestling in a dainty Rococo coiffure, could represent support for the monarchy, but could also be foolhardy in the wrong company. The revolutionary leader Jean-Paul Marat, in a painting by Jacques-Louis David from 1793, is depicted lying dead in his bath, bloodied by the assassin's knife, a white quill still in hand demonstrating his revolutionary role. His lifeless body is white against white turban against white sheet. In a sketch of Marie Antoinette, also by David, the queen is shown with all artifice of youth and beauty removed – *sans* hairpieces, with roughly shorn hair, chemise and small cap with a somehow affecting border of simple goffering, a faint echo of her former taste for finery. She is dressed for the public guillotine, in her underwear alone, her arms tethered behind her, grim-faced and old. Both images are telling and rely for their impact on plain white clothing.

Nonetheless, or perhaps at first because of the frisson of such recent danger it could produce in the wearer, the fashion for Marie Antoinette-style dress continued long after her death, the vogue for simple muslin dresses gathering force across Europe and beyond. Gone were intricate lace collars and fine jacquard fabrics. Corsets were minimal compared with what came before and after. Plain muslin or gauze shawls, or fichus, folded diagonally, were worn as a version of a working woman's neckline, tied behind or held in place in front with a brooch or posy. Men wore long strips of white linen wrapped around the neck and tied behind over a white linen shirt, but otherwise their costume was becoming uniformly dark. Men were increasingly sombre as their womenfolk became more insubstantially dressed, in the male renunciation of fashion. Women's hair was sometimes cut short after the fashions of the *ancien régime* or worn in a raised bun with curls or fringing around the face, sometimes crisscrossed with ribbon, in what was thought of as Roman antique style. Marie Antoinette's softly dressed hairstyle in Vigée Le Brun's portrait of her had been developed when she lost much of her hair after the birth of the dauphin in 1781. It became known as her *coiffure à l'enfant* and was copied on both sides of the Channel. In contemporaneous paintings by Thomas Gainsborough, Joshua Reynolds and Edmund Lilley women's hairstyles are gently bouffant on either side of the head, often augmented with pads of hair, but similarly more natural in appearance. The powdering is retained in many of these portraits even though it had begun to fall out of fashion, as if the artists or sitters were slow to give up the flattering glamour of a dramatically pale coiffure.

In the context of the French Revolution the white linen shift became associated with aristocrats who had been imprisoned during the Terror. So, for those who survived, 'to be undressed in neoclassical muslin in the 1790s was not only to be classical, "natural", and half naked; it was also, especially in Paris, to have been dangerously vulnerable and to have survived.'[17]

After the French Revolution, a chic new fad among the wealthy who had survived was known as *à la victime*, with some young women in Paris in their flimsy white shifts wearing narrow red ribbons, or *fillets*, round their necks as if to mimic the slice of the guillotine. Men, in bare-necked shirts, would leave their hair unpowdered and artfully dishevelled or cut savagely short, as if shorn in readiness for their execution. There was even an exaggerated double-take motion of the head practised at social occasions, as if to suggest being beheaded. Once the danger of execution in the new Republic was allayed, one could enjoy acting brave, much as punk or goth fashions' excesses risk little unless you happen to live in a repressive state where dissent can mean imprisonment and worse. A thin red ribbon or lack of cravat might daringly express danger, but only when the danger had safely passed.

A wife's apparel begins to represent a gentleman's status:
Arthur Devis, *Mr and Mrs Hill*, 1750–51, oil on canvas.

The sometimes ludicrous excesses of the *Merveilleuses* and their
male counterparts, the *Incroyables*, were a passing minor fad, much
exaggerated by those who loved to ridicule an interest in dress, mocking the vastly oversized plumes on their heads and transparent fabrics
that exposed the wearer to the indignity of their natural bodies being
seen by all. William Hazlitt, the English philosopher and essayist,
viewed such excesses as the worst of irrational fashion and didn't pull
his punches. He failed to consider that such exaggerated behaviour
might have been a natural consequence of years of imminent danger

finally being past; one might compare this to post-First World War flapper fashion. Hazlitt entertained no sympathy, reviling them as 'haughty, trifling, affected, servile, despotic, mean and ambitious, precise and fantastical . . . tied to no rule, and bound to conform to every whim of the minute'.[18] So, not for him delight in delicate fabrics and the love of display. The implicit suggestion was that such gorgeous fashions on men, typified by those of the Macaroni Club in London, were wantonly effete and very possibly homosexual, transforming the wearer in his view into a subspecies:

> a kind of animal, neither male nor female, a thing of the neuter gender . . . It is called a macaroni. It talks without meaning, it smiles without pleasantry, it eats without appetite, it rides without exercise, it wenches without passion.[19]

In the nineteenth century, an image by Jacques-Louis David – who had immortalized Marat and exposed Marie Antoinette in her despair – shows Napoleon in a long-sleeved white silk shirt and silk stockings, waistcoat and fitted culottes. Copies of the portrait were widely circulated, and present Napoleon as impeccably dressed, if somewhat creased over the paunch. His style was often less ostentatious than this portrait might suggest, involving relatively unadorned uniforms in line with the officers of his guard, with white shirts and cravats, in marked contrast to the glittering extravagances of Louis XVI's court before him, or indeed of many of the generals in his own army. Like many leaders he understood the importance of sartorial understatement and that maintaining apparently modest dress would best express an identification with the people and lack of desire for personal aggrandizement. The same might be said of Adolf Hitler's dress, for example. Joseph Stalin too chose to wear relatively simple clothing, preferring to wear a pale grey cotton jacket, which became known as the Stalinka. It was a version of the 'French' tunic worn by the Imperial Russian Army during the First World War, though Stalin favoured a less tailored design with an informal turn-down collar. At the First All-Union Congress of Collective Farm Shock Brigade Workers in 1933 he is pictured in a jacket that stands out among the dark and grey suits around him; only the children and women are in white. He rejected outright a smart white uniform designed for him for the Victory Day anniversary of May 1947, preferring not to stand apart from the other marshals.[20] He also chose not to be seen in conventional Western civilian suits.[21] When his jackets needed replacing he was critical of any slight deviation in design, preferring to keep on wearing his old one rather than accepting a garment that had been, in his view, incorrectly made.

There were attempts to portray post-Revolutionary Russia as fashionable and modern. Elsa Schiaparelli was flown to Moscow with Cecil Beaton as her photographer in 1935, to address the prevalent Western view that Soviet women were poorly dressed and did not care for fashion. However, the capsule collection she presented failed to find favour there. Schiaparelli claimed to be astonished by the new Moscow fashion house Dom Modelei. The literal translation of its name, House of Prototypes, suggests a lack of creative individuality that had perhaps encouraged the mockery of Soviet women's fashion in the first place. The designer noted in her autobiography,

> Eclectic mannequins under glass were turning slowly as they displayed rather bewildering clothes. Or at least these clothes bewildered me, for I was of the opinion that the clothes of working people should be simple and practical; but far from this I witnessed an orgy of chiffon, pleats and furbelows.[22]

All the same, the leading Parisienne couturier's understated designs of plain dark woollen jersey dresses with white piqué collars were said to be a disappointment to the target audience. The collection never went into production, an official reason given being that large pockets on the swing coats would have invited pickpockets on the Moscow Metro. Schiaparelli countered that the designs that were being produced were completely unsuitable for everyday life. Yet after years of war, there appears to have been an appetite for sumptuous dress. Dom Modelei picked up on traditional Russian motifs, with colourful floral patterning, tassels and fur Cossack hats, and even the kerchief, which Schiaparelli had roundly disdained. When Christian

Yul Brynner wearing a white Cossack *papakha* in
the film *Taras Bulba* (1962, dir. J. Lee Thompson).

Dior showed in Russia in 1959, the impression made by his elegant
models swanning about on the streets of Moscow and posing in the
GUM department store, on the evidence of photographs taken of female
passers-by at the time, appears to have met an equally unenthusiastic
reception. The history of film is full of Russian-inspired cloche-type
hats, as with Yul Brynner in *Taras Bulba* (1962), distinctive in his
Cossack *papakha*, the soft white sheepskin contrasting with his weath-
ered face. Soviet women in James Bond films are often dressed in white
or pale mink fur hats, the out-of-focus soft underfur and fine, longer
filaments of guard hair together creating their exotic and sometimes
mysterious effect. Fur blurs the edges, as glamorous as a Persian cat.

Modesty in dress, so often considered in relation to women alone,
can be a deliberate device in the power play of politics as much as

in gendered relations. Even when one has lost power but wishes to maintain self-respect in difficult circumstances, a seeming lack of ostentation can be useful. In captivity Napoleon would wear a waistcoat of piqué, or white kerseymere, a fine woollen twill cloth:

> with little figured pockets and short breeches of Kerseymere with flaps and pockets. He never wore anything but silk stockings having a crown at the corner, and gold buckles on his shoes; these were renowned and ornamented with little roses ... he always wore a muslin cravat ... In his room he wore a frock coat of piqué as a dressing gown, pantaloons of white fustian or swanskin with feet.[23]

The log kept by his captors conjures up the ordered life he led on St Helena, with days spent gardening and taking walks, writing letters and drafting his will. His last wishes suggest a precise attention to the detail of dress, listing his 'body linen' thus: '6 shirts, 6 handkerchiefs, 6 cravats, 6 napkins, 6 pair of silk stockings ... 4 pair of white kerseymere breeches and vests, 6 pair of drawers, 6 pair of gaiters.'[24] While leaving substantial monetary bequests to others, his personal property, of which this is only a small part, might have been a disappointment to his son, enjoined by his absent father to see these humdrum items of clothing as precious *memento mori*: 'It is my wish that this slight bequest may be dear to him, as coming from a father of whom the whole world will remind him.'[25] Today, in the auction houses of the affluent world, such items are keenly sought after by collectors, Napoleon having recognized the value, if not the financial heft, of the mundane personal item of dress once owned by an Emperor of France.

The Napoleonic Wars failed to have any lasting detrimental effect on the demand for French fashion. The influence of Marie Antoinette's pastoral dresses continued to spread rapidly across Europe and America. Hooped skirts, if worn at all, were increasingly of smaller size, although the elevated coiffures at first lingered on, on both sides of the Channel. As hairdos gradually shrank, hats appear to have made up for them for a while, as if it were difficult to dispense with the long-established profile of a larger-than-life head. What had been a playful take on the lower-class plain cotton neckline at the Petit Trianon rapidly became more structured and embellished, with intricate starched effects and fine whitework pleats and embroideries, sometimes using openwork techniques or with tambouring and quilting embellished with beads, spangles and sequins. Sometimes designs would be embroidered all over the fabric in satin work or chain stitch. Dresden in Saxony provided some of the most delicate whitework fichus, embroidered with twisted cotton thread on the finest linens, with threadwork or double-layer couching, techniques that were also used on handkerchiefs and ornamental aprons and even men's cravats. Matching 'suits' were made, which might include a cap, sometimes with long streamers called lappets, a kerchief fichu, cuffs and sleeve ruffles. The French master embroiderer Charles Germain de St Aubin derided poorly paid female *Brodeuses en Blanc* and barred them from joining his guild.[26] Despite the enthusiasm for this fine whitework, purchased by the highest echelons of society, their association with ordinary mercers and linen vendors meant that the women embroiderers were not considered to be superior craftspeople. Consequently, they were used as outworkers with no security of employment. White-on-white stitching was hard on the eyes, and professional embroiderers would refer to how many seeing years they had left.

In *The Subversive Stitch* historian Rozsika Parker investigates how whitework embroidery was associated with domesticated feminine virtue. She discusses Mary Wollstonecraft's opposition to an activity that required concentration and skilful application but that could, in her opinion, have little intellectual merit. For women who had no need to work, embroidery was considered a suitably ladylike activity and – unlike music or, worse, reading – could allow the sewer to remain alert to her day-to-day obligations while keeping her family decently clothed. Wollstonecraft insisted that needlework fostered femininity, which in turn harboured the idea of women's intrinsic gentleness, which she considered to be 'a submissive demeanour of dependence'.[27] In Charlotte Brontë's novel *Jane Eyre*, the heroine is questioned by Bessie, her former nursemaid, about what skills she

Children and servant of the British Raj wearing white cotton:
Edith and Isabelle Dunkerley with their ayah, Bombay, 1915.

has learnt at Lowood school, and it is only when she learns that Jane knows how to sew with muslin that she is convinced that she has become a true lady.[28]

The new women's neckerchiefs lent to the silhouette of the late eighteenth century its exaggerated pouter pigeon profile. Hooped petticoats had all but disappeared, revealing the natural line of the body beneath, with a raised waistline that made metal and bone corsets less necessary. Arms were on occasion uncovered and open sandals were sometimes worn to reveal the naked foot, in line with ideas about classical fashion. Soon those in the know were uniformly dressed in white muslin and lawn, imported initially from India and the East Indies. As cotton became easier to acquire and thus cheaper, so the detailed elaborations increased. It was a style that could easily be copied, since it used less fabric and was easier to sew, plus it did not require the same expensively engineered underclothing. However, conforming to the basic requirement of conspicuous consumption, it could still betray the wearer's purse in its lack of, or poorly executed, detail. The style was hugely popular in post-Revolutionary France, worn by Empress Joséphine herself, and in Britain, where it was notably worn by Emma, Lady Hamilton.

In 1788, just before the Women's March on Versailles of 1789, Marie Antoinette's own portrait painter Elisabeth Vigée Le Brun held a supper party where the guests were invited to come dressed as Graeco-Romans, the women in daring loose white tunics.[29] Hamilton, while she was living in Naples in the later 1780s, developed a series of dramatic poses inspired by her husband Sir William Hamilton's collection of Greek vases, which became known as her 'attitudes'.[30] These *tableaux vivants* included classical figures from sculpture and painting. As she posed with her long hair flowing loose or bundled into an Eastern turban, semi-naked in gauzy, draped white robes, the private audience would be tasked with guessing which work of art she was performing.[31] Vigée Le Brun was so taken with Emma that she went on to paint her as Ariadne in 1790, in a white 'classical' gown. This harking back to an approximation

William M. S. Doyle, *Young Lady in a Sheer White Dress*, c. 1805, watercolour on ivory. The young woman is shown in a revealing muslin dress; the miniature was possibly intended as a private love token.

Fine linen pleated collar, Netherlands, c. 1615–35.

of classical dress garnered from statuary and vase paintings Aileen Ribeiro describes as 'aesthetic theory hand in hand with fashion'. She refers to the artist Johann Heinrich Wilhelm Tischbein, who compared a painting of Lady Charlotte Campbell 'to one of the swaying dancers of the paintings of Herculaneum ... [in her] white dress, [and] gauzy scarf'.[32] In post-Revolutionary France officials' uniforms were loosely based on Roman togas, as if the style symbolized citizenship of the new Republic, though the actual designs hardly bear close comparison with ancient clothing.

Plain calico cotton morning dresses and muslins with little puff sleeves all suggest the dress of early childhood. It was a fashion that better suited smaller breasts and undeveloped hips. White silk and satin were worn in the evening, though, as in more recent times and even among the wealthy, older generations are likely to have kept to the more colourful styles of their youth. Among those who were determined to dress youthfully, it could be difficult to give up the underpinnings of their younger years, and the impression of fashionable white dress could all too easily be spoilt by a solid whalebone corset poking through from beneath. Not to have worn such underclothing might have seemed to be disturbingly underdressed for women of a certain age. It has been widely claimed that fabric was sometimes dampened to make it cling invitingly to the flesh beneath, much as in a modern wet T-shirt competition. The source of this rumour appears to emanate from Henri Bouchot, a French art historian, who commented merely that they *looked as if* they had been wetted. Muslins were often embroidered not only with cotton and linen but with silver thread to give them weight and body. This gradual undermining of the new simplicity also included features such as finely worked little ruffs, the edge of a chemise being given an angular Vandyke border, or an upper skirt being looped back much as in an Elizabethan over-skirt, or as in the later more masculine 'English' styles of the eighteenth century. Tucks, frills and cording effects beyond the skill of most home dressmakers came into fashion, and required careful laundering.

In the field of art, fine muslin appears in portraits from the mid-eighteenth century in England, at first over the hooped under-skirt *à la francaise*, as in Thomas Gainsborough's *Mr and Mrs Andrews* of around 1750.[33] Mrs Andrews's gown is in a luxurious silk fabric, in palest shimmering blue, and on her feet are tiny rose-coloured slippers. However, she wears a fine white cap beneath a plain straw hat and the delicate white lawn cuffs, the glimpse of petticoat and the soft white fichu are all reminiscent of Marie Antoinette's *chemise à la reine* pastoral fancies. Mr Andrews wears a fitted white double-breasted jacket, riding-coat style, known in France as the *redingote*, English tailoring becoming sought after post-Revolution. It was a manner of fashion exchange, between Marie Antoinette's pastoral gowns and English hunting, shooting and fishing styles, at a time when the two countries were sworn enemies. Sometimes a feature of dress redolent with qualities associated with someone one considers abhorrent can somehow insinuate itself into our desires. Perhaps it is a way of conquering a fear, of owning what seems initially alien. Or is it merely that our dislike has meant we have attended closely to their image, and we are creatures born to mimicry?

The riding coat was comfortable to wear on horseback, but it also had the advantage of allowing men to show off their figures to great advantage, along with the pale fitted silk waistcoat and tight proto-trousers in off-white wool or possibly buckskin. The reputation of

British tailoring spread across Europe, and even today there remains a market for Savile Row's sober good taste, relying on well-fitting cut and superior fabrics as opposed to runway fashion innovations. The Andrews stand against a backdrop of Arcadian beauty, of the Stour river and the meadowland and open skies of their idealized estate, associating their style with a sense of what is apparently natural, set in highly manicured nature.

In Gainsborough's *Mr and Mrs William Hallett (The Morning Walk)* of 1785, a more intimate tone is set. Painted just before their

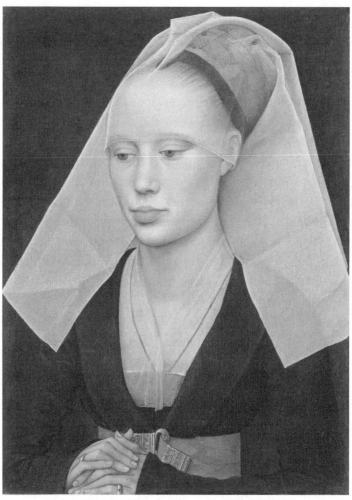

Rogier van der Weyden, *Portrait of a Lady*
(in fine linen fichu and veil), *c.* 1460, oil on panel.

marriage, Elizabeth Stephen is swathed in gossamer ivory silk, the silhouette of the skirt softened and unfocused compared with the Andrews portrait. There are three great white ostrich plumes on her hat, her hair is powdered to match, and around her neck she wears a frilled muslin fichu. As before, the couple are set against an idealized pastoral scene, a sheep looking up to Elizabeth as if to imply she is a simple shepherdess, tending her flock. And yet her clothing is exquisitely beautiful, and William Hallett is following the new fashion for powdered natural hair together with frilled white cuff and linen stock.

In the field of literature, clothing is often left to the reader's imagination, and it is surprising, for instance, just how little information Jane Austen provides about her characters' appearances and especially their dress. And yet, even without seeing one of the many dramatizations of her work, the novels seem to give us a convincing idea of how they look and what sort of clothing they would have worn. We are persuaded to join the carefully choreographed dots. They dress as we imagine such a person of their distinct character might, and the few details Austen does supply confirm the fictive illusion she creates. As it happens, she gives us more specifics than is her custom about muslin and white dresses. The young heroine of *Northanger Abbey*, Catherine Morland, does not know quite what to make of Henry Tilney when he enters a discussion of the pros and cons of muslin with Mrs Allen, who fears that she has torn a hole in her sleeve:

> They were interrupted by Mrs. Allen: 'My dear Catherine,' said she, 'do take this pin out of my sleeve; I am afraid it has torn a hole already; I shall be quite sorry if it has, for this is a favourite gown, though it cost but nine shillings a yard.'
>
> 'That is exactly what I should have guessed it, madam,' said Mr. Tilney, looking at the muslin.
>
> 'Do you understand muslins, sir?'
>
> 'Particularly well; I always buy my own cravats, and am allowed to be an excellent judge; and my sister has often trusted me in the choice of a gown. I bought one for her the other day, and it was pronounced to be a prodigious bargain

by every lady who saw it. I gave but five shillings a yard for it, and a true Indian muslin.'

Mrs. Allen was quite struck by his genius.[34]

Catherine has already had cause to find him 'not entirely serious', but Mrs Allen is impressed with his knowledge:

'And pray, sir, what do you think of Miss Morland's gown?'
'It is very pretty, madam,' said he, gravely examining it; 'but I do not think it will wash well. I am afraid it will fray . . . But then you know, madam, muslin always turns to some account or other: Miss Morland will get enough for a handkerchief, or a cap, or a cloak. Muslin can never be said to be wasted.'[35]

His sister, Eleanor Tilney, whom we gather is to be trusted, 'always wears white', compared with pert Isabella Thorpe, who is not. Jane Austen has no need to tell us that Isabella's gowns are decorated with bows of coloured ribbon and flounces or inset with lace and gilded spangles, all of which were popular passing trends at the time. We read instead that:

Miss Tilney had a good figure, a pretty face, and a very agreeable countenance; and her air, though it had not all the decided pretension, the resolute stylishness, of Miss Thorpe's, had more real elegance.[36]

'Resolute stylishness' seems too insistent on making an impression to be truly graceful. In *Mansfield Park*, Fanny Price worries that her new white dress might be too showy and is reassured by her cousin Edmund Bertram that plain white is a modest choice: 'A woman can never be too fine while she is all in white. No, I see no finery about you; nothing but what is perfectly proper. Your gown seems very pretty.'[37]

White cotton dresses were sometimes within the reach of lower-class women, so that, even if the finest muslins were too expensive, white cambric carefully sewn could make a fair impression of the most up-to-date designs. Nonetheless, white dresses had become so associated with fashion and status that Fanny's aunt, the odious Mrs Norris, thoroughly approves of Mrs Rushworth's housekeeper Mrs Whitaker letting go two housemaids for wearing white, for their sartorial – and class – presumption. A servant was not meant to compete with their richer and betters in fashion. The whole history of sumptuary laws is founded on the need to maintain the social order, an order that could be ably expressed in the class distinctions of dress.

However, when Elizabeth Bennet in *Pride and Prejudice* tramps for miles across the fields to visit her ailing sister Jane, her white petticoats become soiled with mud, causing the two Bingley sisters to call for the disapproval of the men: 'She really looked almost wild . . . and her petticoat, six inches deep in mud.' 'It seems to me to show an abominable sort of conceited independence, a most country-town indifference to decorum.'[38] It seems that even the gentry were expected to show some respect for town superiority over country in matters of dress. If you wore white it had to be kept clean; however, when it becomes dirty, it causes Darcy to confirm, reaffirm, his admiration for Elizabeth's fine eyes; and it is Elizabeth's muddy linen that could be said to expose Miss Bingley's jealousy.

Following the first dalliance with relatively simple white dresses at Versailles, on both sides of the Channel and across Europe and America, younger women, even those of modest means, were opting uniformly for white. Underclothing was principally a white shift to just above the knee. For daywear, a dress or pinafore was worn with a fine half-shirt beneath, the fichu neckcloth sometimes finely embroidered and secured in front, or with longer ties crossed and tied behind the back, veiling a wide-cut neckline or arranged to soften the effect of a higher, possibly drawstring one:

a lawn about the shoulders thrown
Into a fine distraction.[39]

In the evenings the fichu could be left off to reveal the cleavage. An older generation still in heavy silk brocades and velvets must have made a notable contrast in this field of white cotton. The interest lay in the detail of cut of sleeve and bodice, whether embroidered white-on-white floral borders or a Grecian key design were more of the moment. At any rate, as Jane Austen's Henry Tilney points out, muslin, whether it was in unused offcuts or still-good panels cut from a worn-out dress, need never go to waste.

The finds of Herculaneum had made their mark on dress. The evidence they appeared to provide of women's simple white shifts led not only to classical motifs being embroidered onto muslin and gauze, but to new hairstyles that were either shorn or bundled up with little curls arranged around the face. This craze for white dresses revealed more of the natural form of a woman's body. Marie Antoinette may have pre-empted this simpler silhouette, but in the post-Revolution era there was a marked attempt to dress in a style suggesting a classical ideal to represent the new order. Underwear had undergone a marked change, with corsets and cumbersome layers of petticoats left off, as if paring themselves down for a new age, as daring and new as 2,000 years before. There was at first much fun to be had in satirizing the ultra-fashionable Parisiennes in their sheer, often unflattering *négligée*, Isaac Cruikshank in 1799 drawing them with exposed breasts and bottoms even in the depths of winter. However, by the time they were mainstream in England, white had become associated with simplicity of line and more innocent intent. In economic terms, the Revolution had made the import of French silks problematic, and so it made sense for Italy, America and England to turn to relatively affordable and accessible cotton fabrics.

White dress might be affordable for the lower classes, but it could still stand for moral character. In Thomas Hardy's *Tess of the d'Urbervilles*, subtitled *A Pure Woman Faithfully Presented*, Tess's white dress is described as 'her best summer one', but by Alec d'Urberville as 'puffy muslin'. When he abandons her and returns to find her soundly asleep in the wood she is 'pale nebulousness at his feet, which represented the white muslin figure he had left upon the dead leaves. Everything else was blackness alike.'[40] Hardy ruminates on the effect of Tess's rape: she is 'practically blank as snow as yet'.

Fine spun cotton muslin would have originally been imported from India, but in the nineteenth century the invention of the spinning

Lacemaking was a long-established industry in France, as seen
in Nicolas Maes, *The Lace-Maker*, 1652–93, oil on canvas.

mule brought production to England, the raw cotton gleaned from the
American colonies. John Bradshaw of Bolton produced many different
types of cotton cloth, such as cambric, dimity and gingham, that had
formerly been in short supply. English wool provided quantities of
cheaper, lower-grade cloth but had also supplied high-quality fabrics, and this contributed to England's reputation for tailoring. Silk
production was still more associated with Italy and France. Aileen

Ribeiro makes the important point that, in great contrast to our own times, clothing 'took a much greater proportion of income compared to other goods and services'.[41] An additional reason why muslins and whitework came to the fore can be explained by the collapse of the lace-making industry in France. Many skilled workers fled France during and in the aftermath of the Revolution, Napoleon's attempts to revive the long-established trade largely failing.

An investigation of white dress cannot hope to include the wide variety of distinctions in traditional dress motifs across Europe and beyond. Searching for patterns in fashion and non-fashion clothing, there is a risk of failing to notice anomalies and smaller habits of dress. A new habit born in a remote region, but never reaching a city perhaps, is still worthy of being called fashionable within that smaller context. However, Hazlitt reflects somewhat sourly on the democratic possibilities of both the white muslin gown 'now the common costume of the mistress and maid', and the parallel ubiquity of men's dark clothing, so that 'in the grand carnival' of the age, the new fashions seem to him to challenge traditional gender roles:

> Our belles formerly overloaded themselves with dress: of late
> years, they have affected to go almost naked . . . and are, when
> unadorned, adorned the most . . . The women having left off
> stays, the men have taken to wearing them . . . the age is grown
> so picked, the peasant's toe comes so near the courtier's heel,
> it galls his kibe [an ulcerated chilblain]; a lord is hardly to
> be distinguished in the street from an attorney's clerk; and
> a plume of feathers is no longer mistaken for the highest
> distinction of the land![42]

Hazlitt marries the idea of fashion with wider economic change: 'The ideas of natural equality and the Manchester steam engines together have, like a double battery, levelled the high towers and artificial structures of fashion in dress.'

Charles Baudelaire, however, embraces the idea of clothing as part of our aesthetic true self:

The idea of beauty which man creates for himself, imprints itself on his whole attire, crumples or stiffens his dress, rounds off or squares his gesture, and in the long run even ends by subtly penetrating the very features of his face. Man ends by looking like his ideal self.[43]

When fashions turned back again to rich, conspicuously expensive fabrics, those who continued to wear white could look quaint, odd, even deranged. Wilkie Collins's Anne Catherick, in *The Woman in White*, wears white in affectionate memory of Mrs Fairlie, who had once been kind to her, but her white clothing denotes her powerlessness. On meeting her for the first time on a street in moonlight, the narrator Walter Hartright is struck by her strangeness and, in Veblen's aesthetic nausea terms, her ladylike but quaintly unfashionable, un-sumptuous appearance: 'She held a small bag in her hand and her dress – bonnet, shawl, and gown all of white – was, so far as I could guess, certainly not composed of very delicate or very expensive materials.'[44] Fashion has moved on and her simplicity of dress is no longer charmingly innocent but rather invites his sympathy. However, this is in great contrast to Hartright's first meeting with Laura Fairlie, when her modest white makes a very different impression on him, even though the fashion is no longer for pastoral simplicity and her two female companions are far more richly dressed:

> I was struck, on entering the drawing room, by the curious contrast, rather in material than in colour, of the dresses which they now wore. While Mrs Vesey and Miss Halcombe were richly clad (each in the manner most becoming to her age), the first in silver-grey, and the second in that delicate primrose-yellow colour which matches so well with a dark complexion and black hair, Miss Fairlie was unpretendingly and almost poorly dressed in plain white muslin. It was spotlessly pure: it was beautifully put on; but still it was the sort of dress which the wife or daughter of a poor man might have worn, and it made her, as far as externals went, look less affluent in circumstances than her own governess.

At a later period, when I learnt to know more of Miss Fairlie's character, I discovered that this curious contrast, on the wrong side, was due to her natural delicacy of feeling and natural intensity of aversion to the slightest personal display of her own wealth.[45]

It is as if white has retained some of its former religious associations. When the heiress is tricked into changing places with Anne Catherick, she is given Anne's less refined, less well-fitting white clothing to wear, evidence of her new subordination.

This anachronistic white is also found in the dress of Miss Havisham in Charles Dickens's *Great Expectations*. Jilted at the altar years before, she has worn her wedding apparel ever since, representing her refusal to set aside the humiliation of that day. We see her through the eyes of young Pip, who lists her dress in detail:

> She was dressed in rich materials, – satin, and lace, and silks, – all of white. Her shoes were white. And she had a long white veil dependent from her hair, and she had bridal flowers in her hair, but her hair was white . . . She had not quite finished dressing, for she had but one shoe on . . . – her veil was but half arranged.

Shoe and veil increase a sense of there being unfinished business, and even the whiteness of her clothing seems not quite right to the boy. It is white, but not as he thinks white should be:

> I saw that everything within my view which ought to be white, had been white long ago, and had lost its lustre and was faded and yellow. I saw that the bride within the bridal dress had withered like the dress, and like the flowers, and had no brightness left but the brightness of sunken eyes. I saw that the dress had been put upon the rounded figure of a young woman, and that the figure upon which it now hung loose had shrunk to skin and bone.[46]

Later in the novel, when Pip has grown up and comes to realize that he had never been intended for Estella as he had imagined, he visits Miss Havisham at Satis House again. When her dress catches fire, he manages to put out the flames, holding her fast despite her shrieks and attempts to escape him:

> I doubt if I even knew who she was, or why we had struggled, or that she had been in flames, or that the flames were out, until I saw the patches of tinder that had been garments no longer alight but falling in a black shower around us.

However, an hour later, after her burns have been attended to, it is as if the destroyed wedding dress lives on, like the flames that renew in the ancient myth of the phoenix. She lies swathed in white once more, and asks Pip for his forgiveness:

> Though every vestige of her dress was burnt ... she still had something of her old ghastly bridal appearance; for, they had covered her to the throat with white cotton-wool, and as she lay with a white sheet loosely overlying that, the phantom air of something that had been and was changed was still upon her.[47]

In *Jane Eyre*, Mrs Fairfax, the housekeeper, describes the assured and accomplished Blanche Ingram as being 'dressed in pure white'. Later when Jane has the opportunity to see Blanche for herself, we see that her character is anything but pure and innocent. Blanche is proud, mocking the 'more ladylike' Mrs Dent, unkind about Mr Rochester's ward Adèle and dismissive of governesses in front of Jane. Her mother calls her 'my lily-flower', but the lily is associated with funerals and death. And yet Mr Rochester continues to play the part of her suitor, agreeing to sing a duet with 'Donna Bianca', although by now we suspect that he cannot really admire her: 'Miss Ingram, who had now seated herself with proud grace at the piano, spreading out her snowy robes in queenly amplitude.'[48]

The reader is persuaded that Mr Rochester is not interested in Blanche Ingram and so it must follow that her white apparel has nothing to do with modesty or goodness. Jane, in contrast, favours inconspicuous clothing, so that when she is encouraged by Mr Rochester after their engagement to choose lavishly colourful dresses for her trousseau she resists him, agreeing only to 'a sober black satin and pearl-grey silk'.[49] Pearl is the colour of translucence, of glimmering half-light, and is associated with the moon. Jane imagines the married woman she believes she is about to become and finds her new clothing disturbing, as if anticipating that matters may not go well. She shuts her closet against 'the strange, wraith-like apparel it contained; which, at this evening hour – nine o'clock – gave out certainly a most ghostly shimmer through the shadow of my apartment. "I will leave you by yourself, white dream," I said.'[50]

Mr Rochester has managed to get Jane to accept one item of white clothing: an exquisite wedding veil. Later, woken in the night by a terrifying presence in her room, she explains to him what she has witnessed:

> a woman, tall and large, with thick and dark hair hanging long down her back. I know not what dress she had on: it was white and straight; but whether gown, sheet, or shroud, I cannot tell . . . presently she took my veil from its place; she held it up, gazed at it long, and then she threw it over her own head, and turned to the mirror . . . it was a savage face . . . Sir, it removed my veil from its gaunt head, rent it in two parts, and flinging both on the floor, trampled on them.[51]

His mad, bad wife Bertha, down from the attic, presents as a ghostly but substantial flesh-and-blood figure, with white shift but 'savage face' and 'red eyes'. Mr Rochester attempts to persuade Jane that what she had seen was nothing but 'the creature of an over-stimulated brain', but she insists on its dangerous reality, comparing the woman to a 'German spectre – the Vampyre'. Bertha is solid flesh, a figure of threat, but her white garb also associates her with the ethereal, a being of another liminal world. Brontë has the reader addressing both elegantly worn white that is adorned to deceive in the character of Blanche Ingram, and apparently supernatural white that shrouds and comes to expose a dark and ugly secret.

Highly fashionable sumptuous dress and the nightgown worn by a demented woman both rely in their different ways on the effect of their white substance here. Veblen's analysis of dress and fashion unpacks the economic forces that lie behind many of our apparently personal desires with regard to clothing, associating the majority of our choices firmly with the desire for respectability, since 'our apparel

Father and son in dark colours: George Chinnery,
An English Family in Macao, c. 1835, oil on canvas.

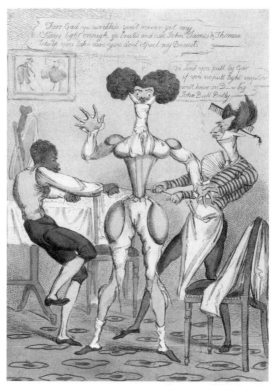

Unknown artist, *Lacing a Dandy*, 1819, etching.

is always in evidence and affords an indication of our pecuniary standing to all observers at the first glance ... more than in any other line of consumption.'[52] This is true of Blanche, but even when Bertha has no status and lacks any sense of respectability, white clothing is empowering, expressing her will, anger and passion as eloquently as any item of high fashion.

It can be frustrating to find how little one gleans about men's fashion in the great novels of the nineteenth century. We may note that male clothing becomes increasingly uniform, and we are forced to redirect ourselves towards female dress. In Paris and to a lesser extent in London, at the beginning of the century, the excesses of men's fashion had begun to peter out. Those of sufficient means were darkly and soberly dressed and looked to their dependants to express their status. However, the influence of George (Beau) Brummell, foremost among English dandies, introduced in effect a style for men that was to survive for centuries and which relied on careful observation and comparison. In contrast to the fops, to the *Macaronis* and the *Incroyables*, he insisted that a man's style should never be conspicuous and that, on the contrary, such an effect was coarse and ungentlemanly. The pared-down apparel of fitted jacket, close-fitting pale pantaloon breeches and undecorated white or pale waistcoat over starched white shirt and neckcloth was intended to make an effortless impression. All had to be fastidiously clean, Brummell going so far as to bathe and to brush his teeth every day. Despite the simplified impression, dressing had become more exacting and time-consuming, and it could take Brummell all morning before he was ready to go out, adjusting the folds just so on the all-important centrepiece of his linen cravat, casting aside each crumpled failed attempt. A mid-nineteenth-century account ridicules the amount of time Brummell took, 'It is not to be supposed that [he] had the neck of a swan or a camel,' and then goes on to describe his attention to detail: 'The head was thrown back, as if ready for a dentist; the stiff white tie applied to the throat, and gradually wrinkled into half its actual breadth by the slow downward motion of the chin.'[53]

Fifty years later and the cravat was only being worn by the country bumpkin squires Brummell had so 'cordially hated.'[54] He disliked rural life and its habits and, it is claimed, people in general, truly fond only of his pet poodles. Today the white cravat is often seen at weddings on the groom and perhaps the best man and gives the impression of the curious contradictory style of austere effeminacy. Lord Byron is said to have most admired two men, Beau Brummell and Napoleon

Jacques-Louis David, *The Emperor Napoleon in His Study at the Tuileries*, 1812, oil on canvas.

Johannes Mytens, *Jacob de Witte, Lord of Haamstede*, 1660, oil on canvas. He is depicted as a gentleman in rich, dark silks offset by a billowing shirt and cravat.

Bonaparte, and as a young man himself adopted the linen cravat. Brummell, for his part, disapproved of Napoleon occasionally wearing black cravats. In Brian Dillon's essay on the cravat, Brummell's apparent simplicity of dress, he argues, suggests a democratization of style that was not born out in practice, but only succeeded in making judgements about income and class more subtle, quoting an anonymous critic of 1818 who refers to 'niceties of attire by which one can spot a gentleman: chief among them, the style of his cravat'.[55]

White muslin and fine linen could filter light, suggesting feminine delicacy, and when worn by a gentleman could make him seem elegant but also curiously effete. 'Its cooling diaphanous textures were an ironic antidote to the labourer's sweat.'[56] White fabric could imply 'impropriety, vanity and superficiality'.[57] Moreover, Alice Barnaby mentions in her discussion of nineteenth-century interior design the way the term 'muslin', or 'a bit of muslin', was used as a synecdoche for women. It was a form of insult, suggesting they wove their mysterious webs to entrap poor innocent men. A more abstract notion of muslin was in tune with theories of the ethereal that had been suggested by Aristotle and endorsed by Newton.[58] Moreover, the fashion for white dresses chimed with the new age of photography. Technical difficulties in focusing lent themselves to the gauziness of fine muslin and the craze for investigating the existence of ghosts and fairies made out-of-focus spoof photographs more easily believable.

The archetypal plain white shirt for men, demonstrating the elegance of keeping it cotton and simple, here promoting an HIV/AIDS campaign.

Using the term 'muslin' as a synecdoche to refer to a woman could also be intended affectionately or at least used as a neutral term, as in Thackeray, when a Mr Huxter enquires with unwitting tactlessness as to whom Arthur Pendennis had been with the previous evening: 'that was a pretty bit of muslin hanging on your arm – who was she?'[59]

The plain white shirt has been a constant feature of male dress for centuries, and its state, whether clean or grubby, could mark a man out as prosperous, respectable, eccentric or having slipped down the social scale. A man down on his luck could seldom present himself in bright white. When grubbiness is read as a bold counter-cultural statement it occurs almost wholly in recent times, when bright whites have become more easily attainable and maintainable. Its intentional form only succeeds when such a choice is not likely to be interpreted as evidence of poverty but as a disregard for bourgeois values.

In the Ealing Studios film *The Man in the White Suit* (1951), Alec Guinness plays a dedicated scientist, Sidney Stratton, who develops an apparently indestructible fabric that can neither stain nor wrinkle. At first the industry and his fellow workers in a textile factory are delighted. However, they soon realize that this will threaten their livelihood and turn on him. Sidney, luminous in his prototype white suit, runs from the angry mob, but as he does so the fabric begins to disintegrate, and the crowd gleefully tear chunks away so that he is left, forlorn, in nothing but his shirt and underwear – which, incidentally, are white, of course. All is not lost, however, for when we see Sidney the following day ruminating on what could possibly have gone wrong, belief in his invention returns as he declares, 'I *see!*' Today it has become possible to produce practically indestructible fabrics, evidenced in the state of our oceans; luckily for the purveyors of fashion, the whiteness of trainers and T-shirts does become less luminous with age, a form of built-in obsolescence, perhaps.

It is not only difficult to keep whites white, but the business of providing beautifully sewn white shirts in the nineteenth and early twentieth centuries was as unrewarding as whitework embroidery, and was even less well respected and paid. It was a job that was often done as outwork, allowing a woman to look after her children and other dependants at the same time. She had often to purchase or put a deposit down on the cloth she was sewing. Thomas Hood drew attention to the plight of low paid sempstresses in his poem about a Mrs Biddell who struggles to support her children on a pitiful wage, and ends up in the workhouse. 'The Song of the Shirt' (1843) was influential in drawing attention to the plight of working women:

Work – work – work,
Till the brain begins to swim;
Work – work – work,
Till the eyes are heavy and dim!
Seam, and gusset, and band,
Band, and gusset, and seam,
Till over the buttons I fall asleep
And sew them on in a dream!

Oh, Men, with Sisters dear!
Oh, men, with Mothers and Wives!
It is not linen you're wearing out,
But human creatures' lives!

White dresses were even for factory work. The woman on the left has a Gibson girl hourglass waistline and white blouse, New Bedford, Massachusetts, 1911, photograph by Lewis Wickes Hine.

Stitch – stitch – stitch,
In poverty, hunger and dirt,
Sewing at once, with a double thread,
A shroud as well as a shirt.

From the sewing machine's first appearance at the end of the eighteenth century, it would take another fifty years before the chain-stitch method, which could easily unravel, was widely replaced by the stronger bobbin-fed machines we use today. At any rate it was beyond the reach of a jobbing shirt-maker to own one, and they tended to be purchased by more affluent homes for domestic use. Machines were gradually improved and incorporated into the factories of the Industrial Revolution, designed for specific tasks to refine the processes of efficient mass production.

Mid-nineteenth-century fashion is dominated by the crinoline silhou-ette, in taffetas and velvets and in rich jewel colours, sombre dark patterns and tartans, with acres of frilly white petticoat beneath. That was during the day, but for the young at least, evening dresses were often pale or of white sat-in, associated with youthful innocence and creating a glamorous contrast with the dark evening suits of the menfolk. In England we see the young Queen Victoria constrained by the new tiny-waisted corseted crinoline, so constricting that a fashionable woman was sometimes quite unable to raise her arms above waist level. Women were held as rigid as wooden dolls with their plentiful skirts impeding a natural gait. Victoria is sometimes claimed to have been the first bride to wear a white

The white wedding dress that set a lasting fashion: Queen Victoria's wedding dress, 1840, cream silk satin with Honiton lace, made by Mary Bettans.

A fancy-dress party at the Residency, Bombay, *c.* 1915.

wedding dress; it was an exception at the time, and its significance is perhaps exaggerated by the long years of black-clothed mourning that were to follow.

Children begin appearing in fashion magazines more frequently, though dressed still as little adults and often only the youngest children wearing white. Filmic images set in that period, such as that of Vivien Leigh as Scarlett O'Hara in *Gone with the Wind*, dressed in white cotton flounces when we first encounter her, can hardly be held as reliable evidence of crinoline fashion. And yet we see Scarlett on her family's cotton plantation, displayed against the idyllic pastoral backdrop of Tara, much as we see Mr and Mrs Andrews in Gainsborough's painting, her image immortalized in the wide-hooped skirt of the crinoline. Look closely and the dress appears to be of fine muslin with lace edging to each tier of her skirt, with short, puffed sleeves and a stand-up ruffle collar, the latter not unlike a simple flounced ruff of the eighteenth century.

The crinoline was uncomfortable and dangerously flammable, yet, like the Spanish farthingale, it had become indispensable to those women in the West who could afford to acquire one. Towards the end of the nineteenth century the Gibson Girl silhouette came into vogue as an ideal of female beauty, strong and elegant with a small waist and magnified bust and hips. Conjured by the pen-and-ink illustrations of American illustrator Charles Dana Gibson, this is no shrinking Victorian violet. She stands proud in a glowing white blouse, with its high round neck and puffed sleeves reminiscent of the leg-of-mutton sleeves of two hundred years before. She is far from the slight girls of James McNeill Whistler's paintings of the 1860s. Whistler's model Joanna Hiffernan is a more vulnerable image, dressed in shades of soft white and often set against a white background, 'in the luxuriance of silks, satins and lace, [providing] the play of texture against texture, shape against shape, form against line', the sole point of colour her red hair.[60] Whereas Hiffernan wears a moderate crinoline,

The elegance of rich fabric in shades of white: John Singer Sargent, *Mrs George Swinton (Elizabeth Ebsworth)*, 1897, oil on canvas.

the Gibson Girl presents a much more confident attitude even though her movement is still severely hampered, and her underpinnings mean that she can hardly sit or indeed stand in comfort. She looks forceful, as resplendent as the figurehead on a ship, but she is constrained by her clothing, by her underclothing.

Palest blue grosgrain silk mantua wedding dress with train,
with white linen lining. The skirt is more than 2 metres (6 ft) wide,
and is supported by large panniers and side hoops around the hips.
Worn for the marriage of Helena Slicher, 1759.

FIVE

Underwear and Dirt

Women's underwear holds things up
Men's underwear holds things down.
Lawrence Ferlinghetti, 'Underwear' (1961)

I used to be Snow White, but I drifted.
Mae West

lizabeth I, resplendent in the finest, most fashionable garments, would not have worn underpants underneath. Her
wide Spanish farthingale petticoat would have had rolls of
padding tied in place to accentuate the hips, making the waist seem
smaller in comparison. All would have been covered in fine white
linen casing. Influenced by French fashion, the farthingale became
more drum-shaped by the second half of the sixteenth century, but it
was only in Germany and Holland that drawers were worn by women.
The eighteenth-century *panier*, a basket-like underskirt with hoops
of whalebone and sometimes with stronger, heavier metal, was held
in place with strips of linen. It is claimed that these skirts extended
out at the sides by as much as 5 metres (18 ft), though this extreme
must surely have been unusual. Doorways, even with narrower skirts,
would still have had to be negotiated sideways, and chairs would have
needed to be armless. A study of the effect of clothing on furniture
design might be productive. It must have been difficult to stroll side

by side with an intimate friend, and a *tête-à-tête* would have been impossible, unless undertaken facing one's partner.

The nineteenth-century crinoline is the hybrid progeny of the farthingale and the *panier*, and became a staple of European fashion, but unlike its predecessors it was no longer reserved for the nobility alone:

> Achieving the right shape depended on the use of stays, known later in the century as corsets, which become an essential feature of a Victorian woman's life from puberty onwards. Not to wear them was to risk being considered a loose woman. It has been estimated that the average corset exerted a force of twenty-one pounds on the organs, although fashionable tight-lacing could increase that to eighty-eight pounds.[1]

The uncomfortable, unforgiving bone and steel couched in linen were covered with layers of frilled white petticoat, a shift or chemise covering the upper body. Men wore a linen undershirt and the shifts of both sexes were cut wider from the fifteenth century. For the wealthy, they were made of finer fabric, sometimes embroidered in whitework. The beauty and expense of such signs of quality made it more likely that the wearer would want to have them at least partly on show, either at the neck or puffed out and escaping below a doublet or from the slits cut in sleeves.

This proximity between the layers of soft and starched muslin, of white overlaying the hidden bone and metal, can seem erotically suggestive, present today in certain corseted bustiers and basques, with their metal buckles and zips and studded dog collars, and even in the ubiquitous underwired bra. The historian Judith Flanders remarks that whereas the Regency cotton shift dress weighed only about 450 grams (1 lb), the excessive weight of the crinoline could mean that a Victorian woman's clothing might be as heavy as 17 kilograms (37 lb).[2] For men, wearing a corset could be shameful, associated more with the ridiculous or the sadomasochistic, as if for a man to be seen altering his physique by such artificial means was unmasculine and embarrassing.

Since the crinoline could all too easily ride or tip up entirely, women began to wear linen drawers, which were at first split, or open, for convenience's sake. Elastic, patented by Thomas Hancock in 1820, soon became used for waistbands and made closed drawers more manageable, avoiding the nuisance of ties and buttons. The wide skirts of a crinoline could get trapped under carriage wheels or caught up in machinery, and were easily set alight by open fires, the glue used in a crinoline's structure being highly flammable. Their shape allowed the air within to intensify the flames, not unlike a hot-air balloon, and a woman could quickly become a burning whirlwind of fire. The numerous issues with crinolines led to many horrific accidents.

However, though the crinoline could be both dangerous and weighty, it did have the advantage of facilitating shoplifting, with the aid of various hooks and hidden pockets. It also provided opportunities for smuggling. One Elizabeth Barbara Lorinz was arrested on a ship returning to England from the Netherlands. She declared that her unusual gait was due to her pregnancy, but was discovered 'to have no less than five pounds of cigars, nine pounds of tobacco, a quantity of tea and a bottle of gin' hidden beneath her skirts.[3] A sure case of crinoline deception.

Punch magazine refers to the fashion for crinolines as 'Crinolinemania', but no sooner was the fashion on the ebb than the publication took to mocking the new bustle, harking back to the false bottom 'bum shops' of the *Merveilluses* of the 1780s. A print satirizes the fashion for enlarged rumps and busts, with the shop proprietor, a certain 'Derrière', displaying his merchandise to a group of women. He attempts to persuade them to purchase the buttock-paddings to help those 'to whom Nature in a slovenly moment has been niggardly in her distribution of certain lovely Endowments', promising to solve any deficiencies by 'artfully supplying this necessary appendage of female excellence'.[4]

The nineteenth-century bustle skirt was advertised as an improvement and it could certainly be argued that it was less flammable than the crinoline, though the underskirt did severely limit ease of movement. It relied on a steel frame patented by Alexander Douglas in 1857. Linen strapping reached down well below the knee, and in

The extremes of women's underwear in *The Bum Shop*,
attributed to R. Rushworth, 1785, etching.

this respect it was more restrictive than the early twentieth-century
hobble skirt shape and, still later, the pencil skirt. Sitting down in a
bustle was awkward, causing an anonymous contributor to the *Boston
Medical and Surgical Journal* of 1888 to be scathing in his criticism:

> The woman in a bustle can never sit down in a natural
> position. It is absolutely impossible for her to rest her back
> against the back of any seat of ordinary construction. I have
> no doubt some of the severe backaches in women whose
> duties keep them seated all day are, due to, or at least
> aggravated by, this disability.[5]

To achieve the most plumped-up behind, some resorted to the
inflatable bustle, and it must have been quite a surprise when one ex-
ploded as Charles Dickens was giving a talk in San Francisco in 1888.[6]
Today's buttock-enhancing pants and accentuating bras sometimes
work on a similar pump system and are thus similarly vulnerable to
an embarrassing and on occasion lop-sided deflation.

Some underwear is discreetly hidden from view, some only ever seen in part. When it is deliberately displayed, underwear's ostensibly private character is often the point. Are there rules in underwear? It used to be widely held that underclothing should never be allowed to show. Glimpsing the back of a prime minister's Y-fronts because he had tucked his shirt neatly in under their elastic waistband was considered by some to be a mark of middle-England prissiness and by others to prove that he was an eminently sensible person, depending on your sartorial politics. When a man wears a vest or undershirt, it has been generally considered right and proper, and essential by the modern well-dressed Italian, for it to be held in place by the underpants, but only ever glimpsed at the neckline. For a man to wear his shirt unbuttoned and loose over an undershirt, *Miami Vice* style, was once thought to be appropriate for the beach alone. Shirts with tails, whether white or coloured, are designed to be tucked in, or so it is argued by the bespoke tailors of Savile Row, Mayfair. To prevent boys from allowing their shirts to become untucked, a 1940s advertisement suggests mothers should sew a band of lace around the edge of their sons' shirt tails, presumably to shame them. Such a thing that would have been unlikely to worry a fashionably appointed man about town in the eighteenth century. In modern dress, the VPL, or visible panty line, when it shows through the outer clothing, has its fans but also its detractors. In Woody Allen's *Annie Hall* of 1977, his alter-ego, Alvy Singer, travels to Los Angeles, having reluctantly agreed to present a TV award. At a party his friend Rob points out a woman as being 'the one with the VPL'. Alvy asks what the acronym means and winces at another example of all he dislikes about West Coast Society. It is not clear

For Mothers Only

To cure boys of the habit of not keeping shirttails tucked in, sew an edging of lace around the bottom of the lad's shirt. There'll be no more shirttails showing.

Lace edging, to embarrass boys into tucking in their shirt tails, from *367 Prize Winning Household Hints from the Armour Radio Show Hint Hunt* (1948).

whether it is the displaying of her underwear or the idea of having a term for it that he finds most distasteful.

Some underwear we might prefer never to be seen by another, such as greying knickers or a favourite but worn-out vest grown soft and tatty with age. In one of Barbara Pym's social comedies a girdle is stuffed hurriedly under a chair cushion, threatening to humiliate the owner when a man she desires drops by. The middle-aged Harriet, in *Some Tame Gazelle* (1950), has fallen for yet another young curate, and since she is in the throes of romantic passion she can ignore the way his long johns are evident beneath his trouser legs. Her sister Belinda is not so forgiving and observes more coolly, 'what a pity it was that his combinations showed, tucked carelessly into his socks, when he sat down.'[7] The curate's unbecoming manner of dress suggests to the reader that he does not deserve Harriet's devotion. The novelist Victoria Patterson remarks on the hidden message of underwear here, which points 'to the powerful forces of loneliness and sexual desire peeking out from under the ostensibly chaste social relations between Pym's clergymen and "excellent women"'.[8]

Harriet takes a great deal of trouble with her clothing and yet, when we first encounter her, her plump figure is dressed only in a Celanese white vest and pants. We are soon put in the picture, informed that she 'liked her clothes to fit tightly and always wore an elastic roll-on corset'. Thus we are presented with the unclothed woman and the buttressed flirt in one. I recall noticing my mother's girdle with its lacy central control panel. The attached rubberized suspenders made red weals on her thighs, and I was appalled. The business of heaving up this unyielding elasticated tube seemed grotesque. At least an earlier style of corset could be hooked up and only later tightened with laces. Was this pull-on variety, I feared, what I too would have to wear one day in order to become a woman?

What Paul Poiret claimed to have dispensed with at the beginning of the twentieth century was still ruling women's lives through the 1950s and '60s. His 'corsetless', often bias-cut gowns in reality required a good deal of restraining underwear beneath them. In the 1960s it was still considered somehow vulgar and unladylike for a grown woman to leave her bottom unconstrained. The fashion historian Elizabeth

Wilson argues that, whereas for centuries the female bottom had been seen as a single smooth cushion, without corseting it became two separate cheeks again, though such natural contours had surely been only too visible through the sheer muslins of the *Merveilleuses*.[9] The sense of freedom for those who lived through that shift must have been extraordinary. My own grandmother, whose heyday was in the 1920s, continued to wear the minimum of underwear – just a silky chemise, loose-legged rayon knickers and cellular vests with satin ribbon straps for when it was cold.

The period of the 1960s and '70s has sometimes been heralded for its bra-free liberation, but perhaps the end of the corset roll-on would be a more fitting tag. Along with many, my mother soon cast her corsetry aside with relief. At first the lingerie industry had produced less uncomfortably tight elasticated over-knickers, maintaining the uni-bottom. Nowadays there has been a further and more successful effort to reintroduce corsetry as reducing and enhancing underwear, and sales have rocketed. Softer and more lightweight Lycra and new breathable fabrics have become available, some formed to avoid the uni-bottom effect and maintain the cleft, and such underwear has persuaded many women back into restricting their bodies. There are whole body suits, with sleeves to the elbow and legs to just above the knee, for that special occasion when one wants to look especially firm and shapely. The underwired and padded push-up Wonderbra, patented in 1955, has been popular since the 1980s. There are now knickers marketed with high padded rumps, their popularity sometimes attributed to the 'Kim Kardashian effect', after the American TV reality show celebrity. In effect, they are a modern-day version of the bustle.

Figure-enhancing underwear is also manufactured for men, with vests to broaden the shoulders and mimic a six-pack, and underpants designed to bolster the genitals. Adverts for these tend to be rather more discreet. Whereas women have more of a choice regarding colour, for men such articles tend to be in white or black alone. In the Renaissance a fashionably minded man might have felt it becoming to wear a generous codpiece, and would have been unlikely to be embarrassed about it. The codpiece was worn on the outside whereas modern enhancing pants are discreetly worn underwear. Codpieces have appeared on the runway of Gucci, but have yet to be worn more widely. On the other hand, a Renaissance man might well have worn a pair of discreetly padded hose to enhance the muscles on his calves, a practice that continued well into the Regency period, when a finely turned calf was still considered fetching, before the looser trouser leg.

The corset's development in all its various guises, for both women and men, gave people the apparent ability to transform their bodies, even to create the illusion that one era had body shapes entirely different from another, suggesting the hourglass figure of the Edwardian age could be abruptly transformed in a generation into the snake-hipped, flat-chested flapper. A fashionable body shape is for all but a lucky few an artifice, achieved by what we wear. Indeed, we are so used to these shifts in body contour that it is difficult to imagine what an entirely natural body shape would be. We cannot help but be persuaded by our particular place in the history of fashion. Some items we find flattering, others not so, and some may seem more natural-looking to us than others, depending on the ideas of a particular moment in time when our tastes were formed. The illusion of an on-trend body-type has rarely been achieved without a panoply of underpinnings, and these have been made largely in white linen and cotton fabric, woven or knitted.

One of the culprits for today's return to so-called shapewear may lie at the door of the rom-com film *Bridget Jones's Diary* (2001, dir. Sharon Maguire), on the strength of a scene where Bridget's large, flesh-coloured stretchy knickers elicit a cry of 'Hello Mummy!' from Hugh Grant's Daniel Cleaver. Bridget had debated whether or not to wear sexy briefs for their date, but the big pants won out, presumably on the basis that if things went that far, it would likely be too late to retreat. 'Absolutely enormous pants!' cries Cleaver. They are the sort of underwear that was considered, since the 1960s, as deeply unappealing, for pitiful virgin spinsters alone perhaps. But the scene brought support pants back into vogue. Daniel cannot easily remove them and that, it seems, is an essential part of their allure. That and some unspecified association with desire for an older generation of forbidden elasticated sex appeal.

As discussions around gender diversity issues become more prevalent, one aspect being addressed by the world of fashion is the need for bespoke underwear to help people to 'outwardly dress for who they are within'.[10] Priya Elan, writing in *The Guardian* newspaper, describes a specialist company's non-binary stock: 'These items include bralettes for those without a bust and packing underwear to create the illusion of a bulge.'[11] From such ideas it might seem that restrictive or merely gendered underwear has become less of a feminist/male-repressive issue and instead its strictures might represent a new sense of freedom. The majority of the company's underwear is black, with fewer white items available, possibly suggesting that, while the style is unfussy and practical, white might imply too great an echo of its binary past. Black underwear is often seen as less conventional, and less something that has to be hidden from view.

For many, long after the corset had fallen out of vogue, there was a reluctance to give up substantial foundation wear. Corsets were familiar and comforting to some, and we are creatures of habit, particularly in relation to what comes into intimate contact with our bodies. Moreover, it must have been a curious and sometimes unnerving experience for women to feel their breasts being lifted and separated by shoulder straps, rather than being supported from below. Some claimed that the lack of familiar support made their backs ache. Even actors who get used to wearing a boned corset during the run of a period play can find themselves missing the familiar support once a run has ended.

Early men's underpants, or *braies*, were baggy drawers and were worn by those of means across Europe. They would have been made of undyed cloth, loose and falling to below the knee, sometimes to the calves, and were held in place with lacing, with the convenience of an open flap or buttons to the front. Wool was thought to harbour lice because of its intrinsic lanolin content, so linen or fustian cloth, a mix with cotton, was usually preferred.[12] Knights would have worn them under their armour to prevent chafing. Those who could afford it also adopted the *chausses* hose to cover the legs, cut on the bias to allow for stretch and held in place with cords. When in the early nineteenth century the fashionable man took to wearing close-fitting breeches or pantaloons, he did not use underpants at all, but tucked his shirt-tails between his legs. Unfortunately, these could bunch up or work free and cause embarrassment, and soon fine-knit drawers for men began to be more widely adopted, in wool or cotton and sometimes in silk.

The intimate parts – breasts, bottom and genitals – are usually hidden or at least masked in our dress, veiled from too clear a view. White coverings are often considered the most modest of options. And yet these private areas of the body have been deliberately exposed from time to time in the history of clothing. In ancient societies the loin-cloth was worn for protection by workers in the field, and primitive brassieres or breast cloths known as *strophium* were worn by female Olympians, as illustrated on vases. However, others, including the wealthy, often wore no underclothing at all. Younger women might use ribbons or cords to lift and draw attention to their breasts, others binding them tight as the flesh slackened.

In central Italy in 1375, there was a law against wearing *pandos*, a type of trouser cut so short that the genitals were frequently exposed. So more shorts, perhaps, than trousers as we know them? Considering the dark style of the Spanish court, it is noteworthy that despite an ordinance of 1623, which limited the amount of trimmings of exquisite white lace, jewels and rich embroideries that could be worn, we see in the portraits of the time evidence that these luxuries continued to be enjoyed, including in those of Philip IV's own family. Perhaps, as in the sumptuary laws in England, such sanctions would not have been levied against royalty. Even with Spanish Catholicism in the throes of the Inquisition, the desire for the fripperies of high fashion still appear to have held fast.

Henry VIII took to the codpiece with enthusiasm, masking but also drawing attention to the private parts, darkly jewelled over the linen padding and under-shift beneath. What had been developed from a plain gusset bag attached to the top of stockings and as pro-tection in armour had become a feature of high fashion. Yet what with a modern eye might seem to concern sexual prowess alone is likely to have been intended to draw attention to a man's ability to procreate, since '"cod" was slang for the scrotum, not the penis'.[13] Soon, many men of the Tudor court were similarly decked out. As well as flattering an important part of the physique, they were convenient for easy urination, and could even provide a useful pocket for small essentials. The new white or pale doeskin pantaloons of the early nineteenth century similarly drew the eye towards the crotch, the effect sometimes augmented by rows of covered buttons.

If someone wanted to look clean and prosperous, they needed to have a sufficient supply of linens. The sixteenth-century commentator Sicillo Araldo makes a direct link between a spotless shirt and proof of good character, insisting that a man 'must have a shirt, beautiful and white, which covers the whole body to demonstrate that he is chaste, pure and of clean conscience, since [the colour] white is clean and pure and without stain'.[14]

When soap, made from lye and animal fat, became more widely available, it remained out of reach of the lower classes until more recent times. A visitor from France in the 1690s finds the use of soap in England worthy of notice, though his somewhat faint praise demonstrates that early laundry soap was less than fragrant: 'All their Linnen coarse and fine, is wash'd with Soap. When you are in a Place where the Linnen can be rinc'd in any large Water, the Stink of the black Soap is almost all clear'd away'.[15]

Araldo's views are very much in line with those of Beau Brummell's 150 years later, who scorned the unwashed, often impossible to launder, elaborate fabrics of his own time, insisting on meticulously spotless linen underclothing, shirts and neckcloths. However, Araldo is also concerned with the virtuous aspect of clean whites, giving even greater importance to a gentlewoman wearing white, since 'the shirt of a woman then must be the purest white and fine, that signifies her honour, which must be white without any stain of vice'.

The whiteness of pre-modern underwear had been valued because it was important to be seen to be clean, and white linen could be boil-washed without damage. Moreover, some dyed fabric could cause skin reactions. Gradually the value of white for practical reasons also came to seem an appropriate choice, associated with moral purity and goodness, and, via the connection with early childhood swaddling perhaps, with innocence. For those who could afford it, this whiteness needed to look not only fresh but preferably as good as new. One

Keeping linen clean required a source of clean rinsing water: Isidore
Alexandre Augustin Pils, *Place Pigalle, Paris*, 1871, watercolour and gouache.

cannot easily backdate oneself but 'a new textile is like a new life, is
clean and fresh . . . a symbol of purity as well as wholeness.'[16]

When white clothing remains unwashed its dirt cannot easily
be disguised. The work of launderers had always been hard, and
they often got a bad press because of their association with bodily
filth. Those who could throw their unclean linen aside and expect
it to be returned to them clean and pressed preferred to put those
who had dealt with their laundry from their minds, much as one
tends to ignore the processes of sewage removal and their hands-on
operatives. Laundresses were often seen as morally lewd because of
this connection with the hidden dirt of underclothing. Even lepers in
medieval England were warned to keep their distance from temptation
in 'the buxom form of the washerwoman'.[17] In sixteenth-century Italy
washing the mountains of linens of the well-to-do meant finding a
source of running water, and rinsing out the soap was also problematic

on account of grime and lye polluting precious drinking water.[18] Art historian Michele Nicole Robinson describes the difficult business of removing ink and wine stains, not to mention the time-worn problems of sweat, blood and other bodily discharges, with various recipes that attempted to avoid damaging the cloth. When collars and cuffs, fichus and ruffles were detachable from a shirt or dress front, then they could become more decorative, as it cut down on the volume of washing, yet fine linen required superior washing skills in order not to damage embroideries, appliques and lace.

So much of the sought-after clean impression of whites relies on their looking and smelling clean. Dark and patterned underclothing can easily appear sordid, even if it is fresh from the wash. That said, grubby and stained whites, from the peccadillo to the murky corners of sexual preference, have their own feral place, more appealing to some than long-worn darks. Erotic fixations aside, a clean but greying bra or time-worn knickers with puckered elastic and stained gusset can be deeply sobering articles of dress.

There have always been those who eschew the necessity to keep themselves clean. For example, James Boswell, the eighteenth-century diarist and biographer, found an unhappy balance between personal hygiene and clean laundry, as he

> seldom washed himself, so that when he was well dressed his clean ruffles showed up the griminess of his skin. He was by no means the only gentleman of the eighteenth century about whom the same could be said.[19]

There are those who lack the confidence to wear attention-grabbing clothing, but still take pride in secret in beautiful, hidden, stored away and necessarily impeccable underwear, a trousseau of sorts that may never be worn at all. An immaculate white shirt is usually partly on show at cuff, front and neck, and marks the wearer out as someone who does not have to get their hands dirty, and who can afford to change their shirt as soon as it shows signs of wear. The caricatures created by Max Beerbohm, for example, of dandified men in extended white collars and cuffs, are aesthetes able to leave the noisome business of laundry to others. The historian David Cecil was impressed by 'the exquisite gestures of [Beerbohm's] trim, deliberate hands'.[20]

As the middle classes increased in number and means in the nineteenth century white linens became a significant marker of success or failure. When fortunes fell and it was not possible to keep one's linen as white as before, hard-won respectability was at risk. A worn, grubby edge of cuff or the greasy tideline on a starched collar could all too easily give the game away. In H. Le Blanc's treatise of 1828 on the cravat, the lengthy title alone suggests how crucial such an indicator of social standing could be: *The Art of Tying the Cravat, Demonstrated in Sixteen Lessons Including Thirty-Two Different Styles Forming a Pocket Manual and Exemplifying the Advantage Arising from an Elegant Arrangement of This Important Part of the Costume.* He mentions a certain German prince in London at the turn of the century, who required 'twenty shirts, twenty-four pocket handkerchiefs, nine or ten pairs of "summer trousers" [white or buff], thirty neck handkerchief [and] stockings *à discretion*'.

Some look away from their tangle of woebegone mismatched items whereas others may take pleasure in examining the contents of their lingerie drawer. Some may even start a collection of the finest items available, such as that of Mary Smiling in Stella Gibbons's *Cold Comfort Farm* (1932). She, we read, apart from her primary hobby of exciting male admiration, has a secondary interest in collecting bras:

> She was reputed to have the largest and finest collection of
> these garments in the world . . . It was hoped that on her death
> it would be left to the nation. She was an authority on the cut,
> fit, colour, construction and proper functioning of brassieres.[21]

In a recent book focusing on women's dress, *Women in Clothes*, the meaning of collections of similar garments is set out for consideration, with photographs of one contributor's eight pairs of white canvas sneakers, of another's eight white nightgowns and another's fifteen pairs of similar white trousers.[22] Yet the more you examine them the more significant seem the most minor features, their uniform whiteness making the distinctions all the more evident. We begin to imagine what might be the considerations that govern their choices of such similar items. For those who consider clothing, who dwell on what they wear each day, the study of others' preferences can be puzzling. Some reasons proffered seem reasonable, relating to a childhood association perhaps or an image that recurs, but others are harder to unpack. If you happen to like white trousers, what makes you want more and more of them, and to retain even those pairs that are old and shabby or now too tight or too loose, and unlikely ever to be worn again? The collections are depicted in grids, and seeing this attempt at neat categorization is reminiscent of looking at white clothing in general, attempting to refine through similarity and then difference.

For those who still use a washing line, some 'smalls' may seem unsuitable to be seen by the neighbours, too comical perhaps, too saucy or possibly too shamefully dull. Some garments may appear disreputable even, stained or simply worn, and thus it is that underwear is often dried inside, away from prying eyes. Clothing can give us away. In a crime novel set in Scotland in the 1920s, suspicion is aroused by underclothing that seems out of keeping for a sheep farmer's wife:

> Next along the clothes line to the splendid underdrawers was a bandeau brassiere in the same white linen with straps of the same type and no Scottish farmer's wife from Gretna Green to John O'Groats could possibly possess such a thing. Not only was it a bandeau instead of a chemise, but a bandeau of a texture and outline that was positively . . . 'Parisien', I said.[23]

If maintaining white clothing and underclothing is tricky, then the means and method of laundry and thus its fabric content is especially important. Even in the context of manmade or blended fabrics, the most expensive underwear is often associated with natural materials, as if South Sea Island cotton, the finest Mongolian cashmere or wild raw silk organza might possess a sense of superior virtue that can impress and raise the status and self-esteem of the wearer. In Veblen's terms, it is because they are evidently difficult to obtain and laborious to produce and maintain. It is not enough for the wearer to know what they are wearing, but it needs to be readable by others, which in part explains how exquisite underwear is often exposed. A narrow hand-rolled silk georgette shoulder strap may require a finely attuned eye to recognize the outlay involved. The middle-ground trademarked label is harder to miss on Calvin Klein underpants, an Adidas sports bra or even Christian Dior 'CD' diamanté-emblazoned tights, but these have perhaps become too affordable to count as conspicuous luxury.

A white T-shirt is likely to have a much shorter life before it is considered worn out than a black T-shirt of similar age, even if the latter is losing its dye and revealing past stains. Historically white cloth has had to be boil-washed, which puts a greater strain on fibres than when using lower temperatures, eventually causing them to rot. In the 1990s Japanese washing machines were more ecologically advanced than in the West, and many washed using cold water alone, relying on advanced washing liquids to shift the dirt. Even so, sheets, towels and white clothing all tended gradually to turn dingy and yellowed. Before the availability of throwaway tissues, it was difficult to get handkerchiefs clean and white again, meaning hours on a slow boil to remove mucus. Washday, even in a household with a spanking new twin-tub machine, could still be a long, foul-smelling business in the 1970s. We are now encouraged to set our automatic washing

Pile of ragged clothing in a migrant tent near Harlingen,
Texas, 1939, photograph by Russell Lee.

machines to short, low-temperature cycles, but the best way to redeem a time-worn white is still to subject it to a soak in bleach followed by a merciless boil wash with a biological detergent. Whether maintaining a bright, bleached and starched cotton shirt or just keeping under-pants from going grey in the wash, advertising campaigns encourage us to purchase their newly developed powders and liquids. They are advertised as softening our water to prevent limescale damage, or including bleaches that are less injurious to delicate fabrics, but they all, we are told, create a brilliant white glow beyond compare.

The business of laundry has long been sold with an almost religious fervour. Liquid bleach, or sodium hypochlorite, was not developed until the eighteenth century. It was used for cleaning surfaces and purifying water, but principally for whitening cloth. Even in the late nineteenth century, after Louis Pasteur's germ theory of 1865, it could still be difficult to convince people of the threat of invisible disease, but everyone could register a greying collar or a dismal stained nightshirt.

Ernest Satow, a diplomat in Japan from 1868 until 1912, describes in his diaries catching sight of a shabbily dressed samurai warrior stripping down to wash in the humid heat of summer, revealing per-fectly white, clean *fundoshi* underwear. Despite the waning fortunes of the samurai, Satow was impressed that the man had managed to keep his underclothing so clean – a sign of self-respect in difficult times.[24] In modern Japan, in *burusera* fetish stores and more openly still in vending machines, used girls' underpants are offered for sale. The word *burusera* is an amalgamation of *buruma*, meaning bloomers, and *sera-fuku*, meaning sailor-suit, the traditional school uniform for girls. In the 1990s it became a profitable source of income for businessmen or perhaps for schoolgirls themselves to sell the girls' used pants, or simply spray new items with vinegar for the same piquant effect; the market was international. Such fetish shops also sold ostensibly worn white school blouses with their distinctive sailor collars and the sort of socks one might see on a small child, so loose they fall about the ankle in charming dishabille.

The more direct contact underwear had with the skin, the more likely it was to be of white cloth. When, for example, women in the nineteenth century adopted coloured petticoats, they were always worn over a white cotton camisole and drawers. The dress historian Alison Matthews David explains the anxiety that grew up around the new aniline chemical dyes when brightly coloured socks in the 1860s caused severe burns, which further supported the idea that white underwear was the safest option to wear. This led to a 'fad for supposedly healthy and sanitary undyed woollen underwear and socks', influenced by 'natural' clothing reforms and the Aesthetic Movement.[25] At the turn of the century the new women's combinations were white, making it possible to boil-wash them. Later, in the Flower Power days of the 1960s, Victorian and Edwardian camisoles were adopted by women as bra-less outerwear, perhaps to suggest the distance the women felt they had travelled since they were used as underwear.

For men, First World War standard army issue underwear on both sides of the conflict was of white or undyed wool jersey. When the Australian Corps reached France, they found little provision arranged for their laundry.[26] Each man had been supplied with only a single spare pair of underpants. The Ordnance Corps had the job of arranging for clothing to be disinfected and deloused, and to negotiate for the use of hotel washing machines, but there were problems drying woollen clothing, particularly in winter. Moreover, each time the combatants edged forward or retreated, new washing and drying facilities had to be organized.

During the First World War, on both sides of the conflict, the unhygienic conditions in the trenches meant that local women had to be employed to wash and mend clothing, hence the wartime music-hall ditty 'Mademoiselle from Armentièrs':

> She got the palm and the *croix de guerre*
> For washin' soldiers' underwear.[27]

When soldiers did manage to have a bath and have their clothing fumigated and washed it did not follow that they had their own items returned to them, or even had suitably sized replacements issued. One account of the consequences of such mix-ups with underwear was recorded at a delousing station in Poperinghe in Flanders:

If you were lucky you got some that nearly fitted you, but, of course, I was the wrong size for that and it would always happen to me that I got huge underwear. They were all Long Johns in those days, and by the time I'd done them up they were right around my chest, and I'd also have to take about three folds in the bottom of the legs. That would be topped with a vest hanging down to my knees. On the other hand, a fellow who was a six-footer would be issued with a set so small that he could hardly get into it at all, so we had to swop as best we could.[28]

Clothing was recycled, often taken from the dead or at least from what had been discarded on the battlefield. When it was too far gone to be worn again, the woollen waste was sent home and remade into blankets. However, this association with death and corruption made wool that had not had this gruesome history seem much more appealing, hence the label 'Pure New Wool', a term first used to denote its non-battlefield origins.

Women joining the Russian Battalion of Death from 1915 were issued with underwear, often for the first time in their lives. Similarly in the British Women's Army Auxiliary Corps, although it was assumed that the women would provide their own underwear, often poorer recruits had no experience of such garments, since 'knickers were an upmarket item'.[29]

Just as women's breasts are often the focus of attention in dress, similarly male genitals and bottoms have rarely been wholly disguised, even in the darkest days of renunciation. In the 1990s a fashion emerged among young males, initially men of colour, for low-slung trousers, which exposed to varying degrees their sparkling whites, referred to as 'sagging' or 'low-ridden', to a point below the bottom cheeks and so requiring constant hitching up to stop them from falling down altogether. This was a potentially subversive street fashion that ignored the irony of its promotion of certain mainstream underwear labels; however, as the practice became more popular, all colours and less expensive brands of underpants began to be worn. The trend has sometimes been linked to prison garb, as if the wearer had had their belt confiscated by the guards, or a sexual preference. Many enjoyed the look simply because they recognized an older generation could not carry it off. President Obama spoke out against the low-slung fashion. Several American towns even attempted to ban the 'hang-low' style, but rather as previous sumptuary laws were bound to fail, it proved a tricky business to enforce. In 2013 the mayor of Pikeville in Tennessee cited the authority of a Dr Mark Oliver Mansbach of the National American Medical Association (NAMA) in his campaign against the droopy drawers. Mansbach's study, the mayor explained, proved beyond doubt that '8 out of 10 "saggers" suffered from sexual problems like premature ejaculation.' Unfortunately for him, neither Mansbach nor the NAMA existed. Pikeville's mayor had failed to grasp that the information had been nothing but an April Fool's joke at his expense.[30]

Just as items worn as underwear were more or less uniformly white until the twentieth century, both because it made laundry easier and on account of an association with the prized notion of purity, so clothing worn for sleep has also been almost entirely white. Designated nighttime attire was only for those who could afford it, the majority going to bed in their under shifts and/or daytime shirts. Nonetheless, by the end of the eighteenth and early nineteenth centuries even a servant might have been expected to wear some sort of nightwear and, in the prudery of nineteenth-century Europe, it would have been a necessary item for all would-be respectable females. For the more affluent, there was the possibility of night caps, perhaps embroidered white on white, and tasselled or with pom-poms swinging.

If underclothing is there to protect the outer clothing from urine, faeces, blood, semen, sweat and all bodily excretions, then it follows that it must at times harbour such naturally produced filth. Underwear's traditional white fabric represents our desire to deny this unavoidable fact of life. A baby fouls itself and a parent or carer removes the nappy and replaces it with one that is fresh and pristinely white. A brown or tan fabric would be more practical, but white is preferred because it demonstrates not only cleanliness but good parenting. In great old age, too, those who are well cared for are often clothed in white, in hospital gowns and snowy incontinence pads, as if to demonstrate their return to a state of guileless innocence. Many West

Catherine Deneuve in impeccable white underwear as
Séverine in *Belle de Jour* (1967, dir. Luis Buñuel).

Coast retirees in America adopt white and pastel-coloured romper-
like cotton jersey or fleece suits and white trainers reminiscent of a
baby's bootees, as if reverting to the jolly innocence of early childhood.
A generation ago, if you were to attend a theatre matinee in England
and look about you as the lights were dimmed, the audience would
have seemed a sea of glimmering blue-white acrylic patches in the
gloom, the white shawls of the retired ladies all aglow. Today older
people of both sexes are just as likely to wear trainers and sportswear
to the theatre.

Although not all underwear is white, it remains a marker of
cleanliness and sometimes personal integrity, and its flip side is one
of potential defilement, of what is transgressive. On the other hand,
images that are entirely innocent of pornographic intent can easily
be interpreted as connoting sexual deviance. The love of impeccably
clean whites can in itself become a fetish, becoming 'implicitly associated with both filth and eroticism'.[31] Catherine Deneuve, as a beautiful
bourgeois woman unable to respond to her husband sexually, wears

expensive and perfectly unsullied white underwear in Luis Buñuel's *Belle de Jour* (1967) as she works in secret as a prostitute in a high-class brothel. The writer Aritha van Herk reminds us of the evidence that laundry can betray, of semen stains and blood, since 'Laundry persists as a metaphor for secrets, and tied to its degenerate reputation is laundry's implicit association with the erotic.'[32]

In soft pornography, a common means of tastefully disguising erotic intent is to dress the participants in underclothing that is un-impeachably white, suggesting that which is wholesome and good. In both hetero- and homoerotic advertising white underclothing is a safe haven, neatly undercutting and at the same time drawing attention to potentially sexual suggestiveness, of a whiteness that can all too easily be breached and dirtied. The modern-day's ubiquitous black underwear, while it may be marketed for its sophistication, is more likely to be chosen by most people for its practical qualities, because it can hide the evidence of staining and wear and is also in tune with the widespread vogue for black outer clothing. Even when a person does not bother with washing their body much, putting on fresh and preferably white underclothing that would otherwise 'show the dirt' can help dispel the impression of bodily filth. What the writer Quentin Crisp claimed of dust – 'There is no need to do any housework at all. After the first four years the dirt doesn't get any worse' – some believe to be true of their bodies.[33] If left to their own devices, dispensing with soap and other unguents and perfumes, their bodies will somehow manage their own more natural cleansing process, reaching a constant but acceptable state of individual animal odour. This approach can hardly be applied to the upkeep of white underclothing.

SIX

Meringues and
Sleek Satin Shifts

Lawn is for a bishop's yoke;
Linen's for a nun;
Satin is for wiser folk.
Dorothy Parker, 'The Satin Dress' (1926)

In an advertisement of 1987, the virtues of Ariel Automatic washing powder are extolled for getting white dresses immaculately clean at low temperatures. Delicate nylon fabrics cannot survive a hot wash, as the owner of Janice Smith's Bridal Hire shop affirms:

The things that happen to my bridal gowns! Like mud on
the hem. Even Beaujolais down the front. It all comes back
home and unless I get the dress totally clean I can't hire it
out again. My gowns are delicate so they have to be washed
in low temperatures . . . With an Ariel wash it's so clean
it sparkles. The bride feels she's the first girl ever to wear
the dress!

It seems that a wedding dress should feel brand new. The ambition of many a young woman is even today to wear – rather than take – the veil. The archetypal bride remains a figure in white in the imagination, fragile in tulle and lace, seductive in clinging bias-cut

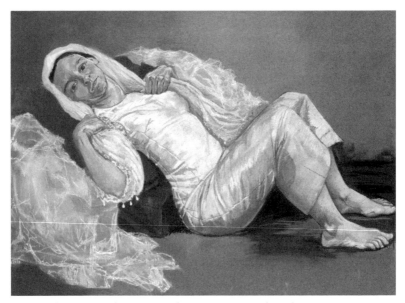

Paula Rego, *Bride*, 1994, pastel on paper mounted on aluminium. Rego explains that the 'hands and feet are uncovered [because] it was so vital that her extremities were exposed as they are in all animals'. The white satin and veil, conventional symbols of marriage, are creased and crumpled.

crêpe or a rustic fantasy in billowing cotton voile, each all too easily sullied. A bride must look untainted by stain or dirt. She stands for virginal innocence with the promise of sex to come, and the white dress and veil may even perform a magic trick, making her feel intact all over again.[1] Like a future princess walking down the aisle of a great cathedral, she is expected to be unmarked by experience. Do women still yearn to become a radiant bride, honoured and admired? As a child I assumed that one day Prince Charles would ask for my hand in marriage. I was a little hazy as to how this was to come about, since my family did not mix in royal circles. Later, it came as no very great surprise that my friends had harboured similar expectations, but about themselves. It was not that I was keen on the idea, but it was a duty, and each of us was prepared to be the chosen one – until the age of about eleven – and to don the white fantastic in our country's service. As we had all come across images and films of glamorous society weddings, it seemed only natural that we would one day receive our share of admiration.

Many may harbour the secret fantasy of a dress that will transform them like Cinderella at the ball, if only for a day. When romantic love is triumphant, when we are at last adoring and adored, a happy future assured, such a moment is often represented in the mind's eye by a dress of luxurious and ephemeral white, which in actuality is probably restrictive and uncomfortable. Nearly always this dress is of a bygone style, as if marriage harks back to the past, the virgin bride hampered by her skirts, her delicate shoes and veil, all declaring her need of a husband's protection. As a by-product of this happy event, everyone, family, friends and even enemies, will surely be amazed to discover our previously hidden grace and beauty, if only for a day. Photographs of this momentous event will sustain us into the future. That is the theory, and despite the countless counter-arguments and counter-examples available, even to my friends and me way back then, from feminist and puritan position alike, it is remarkable how strong the desire for a white wedding remains in so many cultures across the globe.

Today's media has managed to advertise the cachet of the white wedding gown to such an extent that even when more local traditions are maintained, a bride may still choose to have or hire another, secondary dress in white, an image which she can then disseminate across social media. In China, where red is traditionally worn for weddings to symbolize prosperity – and the ceremony is even called the Red Event as opposed to the White Event, which is a funeral – some brides nonetheless opt to quick-change into a Western-style white dress for their official photographs. These may be radically different from their embroidered, richly colourful traditional gowns,[2] even as chic as a white trouser suit, as *outré* as a feathered mini dress with beak attached.

The history of the white wedding dress is relatively recent. It is not that white was never worn by a bride – indeed sometimes it was worn by both bride and groom – but it only came to be an essential feature for brides after the wedding of Queen Victoria in 1840. Dress historian and curator Edwina Ehrman has the first documented white wedding as being Philippa of England's marriage to Eric of Pomerania in 1406, when she is said to have worn a white tunic with a white silk cloak, bordered with squirrel and ermine fur. Mary, Queen of Scots, married Francis, the Dauphin of France, in white, despite it being the traditional colour of mourning in France. The custom for many royal marriages across Europe as well as in the East had been to opt for the sumptuousness of red, but Victoria happened to choose cream silk satin over her hooped crinoline petticoat, with fine off-white Honiton lace at neck and sleeve. She was small and childlike, with elfin features and a tiny waist, all of which contributed to the ethereal quality of her appearance. She was a fairy queen amid the many dark and uniformed men that surrounded her, along with the colourfully attired representatives of foreign royalty and the nobility. Beside her new husband in his scarlet and gilded jacket, she represented the pure, innocent young bride.

Victoria held a position of great influence at the height of the British Empire, but the success of the white wedding dress must be partly an accident of time, when her image could be so easily spread to all quarters via the wonders of photography. The notion of a bride in white effectively grew more significant than the particular individual involved, even a queen empress.

The young Victoria recorded in her journal on the morning of her wedding day:

Mama brought me a Nosegay of orange flowers [white orange blossom]. My dearest kindest Lehzen gave me a dear little ring. Wrote my journal, and to Lord M. [Lord Melbourne]. Had my hair dressed and the wreath of orange flowers put on. Dressed. My wreath and veil were thus worn ... I wore a white satin gown, with a very deep flounce of Honiton lace, imitation of old. I wore my Turkish diamond necklace and earrings, and my Angel's beautiful sapphire broach ... my twelve young Train-bearers were dressed all in white with white roses, which had a beautiful effect ... The Ceremony was very imposing, and fine and simple, and I think ought to make an everlasting impression on every one who promises at the Altar to keep what he or she promises ...

Later, when she returned to the palace, she described what she wore alone with her new husband: 'undressed and put on a white silk gown trimmed with swansdown, and a bonnet with orange flowers'.[3]

Here are the contrasting calls of public duty and personal romantic feeling. The various keepsakes, old and new, borrowed and blue, from her mother and her governess-companion Louise Lehzen are forerunners of today's bridal and bridesmaids' gifts. It had long been customary for items to be handed down or lent, often from a bride's parents, on her wedding day, which reinforces the solemnity of the occasion.

Queen Victoria could certainly not have foreseen how the idea of marrying in white was to gather force because of the impact of her own choice. And, in any case, a white dress was a perfect contrast to the dark background against which Victoria and her husband were memorialized in the official (black-and-white) photographs of the event, the Spitalfields silk satin picking up the light, the Honiton lace veil and flounce filtering and diffusing and making more mysterious the sumptuous effect.

In 1914, when Elizabeth Bowes-Lyon married the Duke of York, the future George VI, a film of the occasion was made available and widely shown in cinemas. The new queen's fashionably simple shift-shaped dress in ivory chiffon moiré, embellished with bands of pearl and silver lamé, were designed by the court dressmaker Madame Handley-Seymour. The bride's veil was held in place by a bandeau and clasped to each side of her face in the manner of a silent film star, a look that closely resembles a medieval European fashion. She wore a white ermine cape given to her by the king, and her antique veil and train was lent to her by Queen Mary. Today it is more often the wedding of a film or reality-show star, or a popular television presenter, that is likely to be minutely studied and replicated. However, the marriage ceremonies of Diana Spencer and Catherine Middleton attracted huge worldwide television audiences. It is as if the idea of royalty, of a class apart from ordinary possibility, has retained its appeal to the aspiring imagination, with its dynastic continuity suggesting a safe happy ending.

A fairy-tale concoction in yards of diaphanous veil and train, the wedding dress more often exemplifies the style that is seldom entirely of its era. The neck frill and puffed sleeves in raw silk of Diana's dress, designed by Elizabeth and David Emanuel, takes us straight back to the 1980s but perhaps also to an earlier time, to the image of Marie Antoinette in her flouncing shepherdess garb. Catherine Middleton's gown, in contrast, with its plain ivory satin and its sleeves and neck of handmade lace, is more restrained. It recalls the simple lines and luxurious fabrics of a Renaissance robe; her sister's bridesmaid dress is in comparison streamlined and more contemporary, but the flattering silhouette inadvertently threatened to steal the show. Bridesmaids are meant to enhance the impression of the bride but, if they are of the bride's age, they should not appear too attractive. The fashion historian C. Willett Cunnington mentions a society wedding in 1901 where the bridesmaids were dressed in black, perhaps to draw attention away from the bride, or possibly to make her stand out all the better.[4] Middleton's dress was widely described as modest and traditional rather than fashionable, and certainly not edgy. Perhaps that was the point. She appeared understated and safely conservative in her style as she joined a long-established institution.

Meghan Markle's wedding dress was markedly plainer than her sister-in-law's. The sleek, minimalist silk gown without lace or adornment was cut straight across from shoulder to shoulder. It was created by Clare Waight Keller, at the time artistic director of the Parisian house of Givenchy, and created an immediate impression of elegance and worldly sophistication. And yet it is Middleton's choice that appears to have made the greater mark. It is similar in style to Grace Kelly's iconic wedding dress of 1956, another commoner magically made royal. Middleton's dress may be beautiful, but it is also uncontroversial, nostalgic and not obviously sexy, despite the deep-cut neckline. In commercial terms, it brought its creator, Sarah Burton, and the fashion house for which she worked, Alexander McQueen, much greater prominence – significantly a British brand and an English designer. Of course, it is the Duchess of Cambridge's future role as queen that contributed to the attention she was given, but had she chosen a more avant-garde style it might well have been found less appropriate, to use that weasel term. A future queen's wedding dress, and perhaps that of any bride, is meant to conform to some idea of tradition in which sexiness is only a minor contributing factor.

Queen Victoria planned to wear her wedding dress on subsequent occasions, and many women choose to dye or cut theirs shorter to get more wear from a dress that is likely to have been costly. Others prefer to swathe their dress in acid-free tissue and hide it away. Perhaps it is with the intention of a daughter wearing it one day, or just for the pleasure of hoarding and unwrapping it from time to time to revisit the memories it evokes. Without this habit of archiving, we might never otherwise have the opportunity of seeing such precious items from the past in good order. Moreover, it brings about the wedding dress's transformation into a magical ritual garment. When the wedding of a celebrity is not publicized, as in the case of actor Carey Mulligan's in 2012, there is speculation in the popular press, impressed perhaps that offers for exclusive coverage have been rejected. However, the rumours that Mulligan wore Prada together with Wellington boots created its own lyrical impression.

When a woman has been married before there lingers a view that she should abstain from wearing white again, even if widowed and certainly not if divorced, suggesting a connection with both virginity and sexual monogamy. Off-white or preferably a pastel colour is said to be more appropriate. Some say that a bride, and certainly a bride dressed in white, should not be obviously pregnant; others that so long as it is the groom's progeny, then it merely fast-forwards the whole thrust of the occasion. Nowadays such rules are largely ignored, though it is still considered tactless for a guest at a wedding to wear white, in case it might steal the bride's limelight. The then Duchess of Cambridge was denounced in some news outlets for being in white on Markle's 'big day', although her coat and hat were in fact pale primrose yellow, but obviously, for those on the hunt for possible scandal, far too white a shade of pale.

In Imperial Russia, it was not only the bride's dress that was white but, importantly, the night clothes of the bride and groom on their wedding night. This was again a symbol of innocence and purity, although the costume curator Nina Tarasova suggests that the wearing of white has particularly solemn connotations in Russia.[5] The wedding dress of Alexandra Feodorovna in 1894, in line with the traditions of the Romanovs, was in silver brocade with a white satin lining, designed by Olga Bulbenkova of the Madame Olga atelier. Precious silver in all its lustrous subtlety is whiteness in metallic form. Incidentally, when fabric is infused with silver it can deter the growth of bacteria on the body, and is effective against lipid-enveloped viruses, such as coronavirus.

During both world wars shortages of suitable fabric, and a sense that it was in poor taste to wear a luxurious dress in a time of tragedy and death, inhibited the holding of white weddings. Moreover, marriages often had to be hastily arranged during leave, causing Dorothy Parker to quip: 'It takes two to play a Wedding March – one plays "here comes the bride" the other "there goes the groom".'

Like their men, many women opted to wear their uniform or war-related work clothing for their wedding as a point of pride, to show their commitment to the war effort. Sometimes there might be a nod to the importance of white, with a sprig of heather or a posy of white flowers. Many a bride during the First World War would have been wearing formal mourning for lost relatives, even for a former husband who had recently died, and so could hardly have worn white.

Those who managed to arrange a more formal occasion were at least assisted during the war by the new pared-down fashions, which needed significantly less material. In 1916 *Vogue* recommended an approach suitably 'serious and discreetly gay' that featured narrowly cut shepherdess wedding gowns and medieval-style tunics with drooping Rapunzel sleeves and jewelled girdles like Lady Greensleeves herself.[6] Tiny covered buttons down the back suggest the bride would need the assistance of her groom to unbutton them on their wedding night. Nostalgic styles are particularly evident during both the First and Second World Wars, as if the designs from the past must have held some comfort and reassurance. Like a baby being christened in a handed-down dress, wearing a mother or grandmother's wedding gown upheld a sense of continuity during uncertain times.

It was hard to acquire, but when a silk or nylon parachute could be obtained, it must have seemed suitable material for wedding gowns both because of its origins – being of the war – and because it could be adapted into something that symbolized the future. Its material qualities of delicate semi-transparency and luxury suit such romantic

The mysterious subtleties of silver lamé: Marguerite Agniel, actress, dancer
and beauty guru, in supple form, *c.* 1929, photographed by J. de Mirjian.

optimism and so it is hardly surprising that wedding dresses of this
fabric became some of the most treasured of the Second World War.
Parachute silk was only available as surplus due to some fault that
had made it unsafe to be used in action, or sometimes it could be
garnered from a pilot after he had parachuted down. Bride-to-be Lois
Frommer managed to incorporate a 'U.S. Army' logo and stencilled
serial number into her dress that was fashioned from a cream silk
chute, joking that it 'makes it look official' (and very much in line with
late twentieth-century on-show labelling).[7] A photograph of Bergen-
Belsen survivors Lili Lax and Ludwig Friedman was taken on their
wedding day in a displaced persons camp, though the dress went on
to be worn by many more brides:

> Lili told Ludwig that she had always dreamed of getting mar-
> ried in a white dress, so he obtained a white rayon parachute

Tiered white wedding dress made from a parachute, 1945–6, silk and nylon.

from a former German airman for 2 pounds of coffee and
cigarettes. Lili used her cigarette rations to hire a seamstress,
Miriam, to sew the gown. Miriam used the leftover material to
make a shirt for Ludwig . . . Six months later, Lili's sister wore
the gown when she married, and then their cousin Rosie wore
it. Lili lent the dress to many more brides.[8]

When traditional fabrics were hard to find, other even less likely
materials were used, such as recycled sheets and net curtains. Even
upholstery was reused in place of brocade.

In the West grooms have customarily donned a morning or
dinner suit (or tuxedo) in which to get married. Recently, white and
pale grey have been adopted, as well as less formal styles of suit that
can be worn again at other times. In the field of fashion for men,
designers produce suits that set out to flatter the shape of the male
body just as wedding dresses are intended to enhance the form of a
bride. Wedding suits are often deliberately tight-fitting, sometimes
acting as a form of corseting, accentuating and flattering the figure
beneath. Such male outfits often have numerous white accessories,
from shiny top hats to cummerbunds, silk satin ties and blooming
silk pocket handkerchiefs. Co-respondent-style brogue shoes might
be in cream-lacquered kid leather, or the colours can be reversed,
so that the main body of the shoe is black, with the heel and toe cap
white – a deliberately extravagant choice with the colour most easily
marked in the most vulnerable position. If you have ever worn a pair
of pale suede or velvet shoes, then you are likely to appreciate the tense
pleasure of such choices. It is a luxurious white risk.

Nigel Lythgoe with his dance group, 1976, photograph by Allan Warren.

SEVEN

High Fashion and Street Fashion

'They give Robin such confidence,' said Kit.
'I'm sure white boots have a psychological effect.'
Jill said, 'An elderly actress once told me much the same thing. She was showing me a photograph of herself during the First World War, with white boots up to her knees, and she said, "My dear, when I'd me white boots on I could have kicked God's throne from under him."'[1]
Dodie Smith, *It Ends with Revelations* (1967)

I f white is a colour in clothing, it is the lightest colour, sometimes called colourless, achromatic, hue-less. It may remind you of fresh fallen snow, of the opaque liquid quality of milk or of chalk gleaming bright in the dark earth. It can reflect and scatter all visible wavelengths of light. When all colours in the spectrum are combined, in theatrical lighting and on your computer screen, it becomes pure clarity, just as moonlight dispels all other colour but white. It is no wonder then that couturiers and dressmakers, the fashion-obsessed and even the modest dresser who simply wants to demonstrate that they are plain and clean, all call on the qualities of white. The photographer and the portrait painter solicit whiteness to achieve the impression of both depth and highlighted proximity, and these qualities are relevant in how we may come to view the colour of our clothes. Cricket-playing nations, for instance, wear white for Test matches, a vivid contrast with grass and ball, but also representing a tradition of all-white uniform that has been maintained since the 1800s. More generally, in the complex range of whites and their near neighbours – cream, watery opal, shadowy greys and silver, palest blue, vanilla, rose and peach-tinted whites – they may be in a state that is either brilliant or bleached and washed out. Each nuanced hue may suggest subtly different associations, the impenetrable and the fragile, and all in turn affected by their colour context.

Is a degree of daring or self-confidence required to wear white boots, say? Is there perhaps something intrinsic to whiteness that can affect us, that can make a tricked-out bride or a child in a brand-new judo kit feel omnipotent? Perhaps when worn as arctic camouflage uniform this would be less the case, when a snow-bound whited-out backdrop must lessen the impact of white. White is uncompromising for reasons of its impracticality and its powers of light reflection, but it hardly belongs to the domain of high fashion alone. It can read as pure, basic, clean, holy or just commonplace, but can also be elitist or seem expensive. It is seldom dull, rarely goes unnoticed, whether perfectly fresh and clean or soiled and worn out. It can cut a dash on the catwalk, often in the final act of a grand collection, with the tallest, haughtiest bride model contrasting with the simplicity of her pure white dress. She high-steps out in strobed splendour in the dazzling denouement, perhaps followed by a shimmering bevy of bridesmaids. The designer edges onto the stage after them, head bowed, more often in contrastingly humble dark clothing, symbolizing their role as creator. They are like the darkly dressed male head-of-the-household as described by Veblen, his dignity and status expressed through the clothing of his dependents, his womenfolk in particular: 'Propriety requires respectable women to abstain more consistently from useful effort and to make more of a show of leisure than the men.'[2]

Yet back in the most hallowed ateliers of Paris, where the craft of fashion is perhaps at its zenith, the sewers are almost entirely women and wear their pristine white coats as a badge of office. They are a far rarer breed than the scientist, medic or dentist. They labour on tables padded, shrouded, in plain white sheeting and there they make up toiles in cambric as sample garments, at the first material stage of bringing a designer's ideas to life. These apparitions, of artisan and the

The simplicity of a white dress: John Constable,
Mary Freer, 1809, oil on canvas.

The lustre of silver and the simplicity of white lawn: Joseph Highmore,
Mrs Sharpe and Her Child, 1731, oil on canvas.

'Classical' white of a modest cut: Baron François-Pascal-Simon Gérard, *Alexandrine Émilie Brongniart*, 1795, oil on canvas.

Shades of white dress against a white background: James McNeill Whistler,
Symphony in White, No. 1: The White Girl, 1862, oil on canvas,
the title suggesting a parallel between music and the artist's work.

Self-portrait of Polish artist Jacek Malczewski in traditional
artist's smock with cravat and beret, 1914, oil on canvas.

Sheer white clothing reveals the flesh beneath:
Albert Joseph Moore, *Lilies*, 1866, oil on canvas.

Ernst Ludwig Kirchner, *Girl in White Chemise*, 1914, oil on canvas.

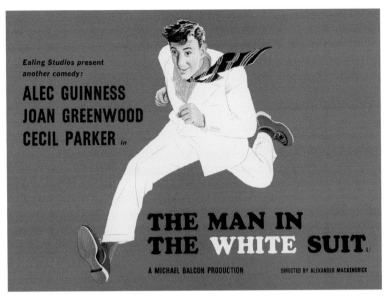

Poster for *The Man in the White Suit* (1951, dir. Alexander Mackendrick), featuring Alec Guinness in a seemingly indestructible white suit.

Annet Couwenberg, *Dutch Ruffled Collar*, paper doilies, fabric, boning, wood and flocking, installation view at the 'Radical Lace and Subversive Knitting' show, Museum of Arts and Design, New York, 2007.

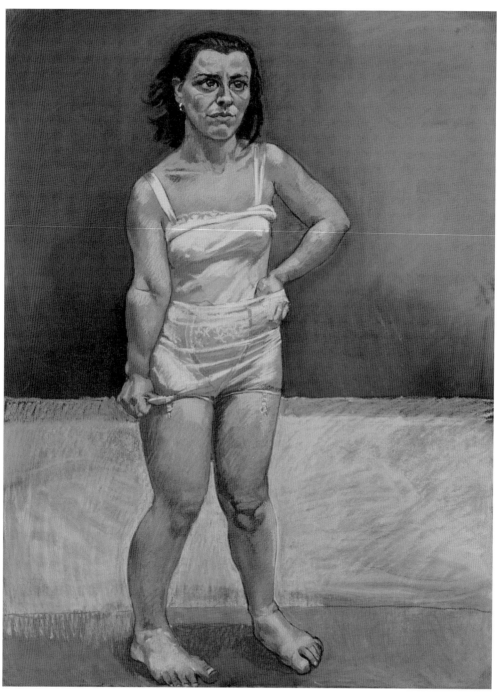

Paula Rego, *Girdle*, 1995, pastel on paper mounted on aluminium.

modelled toile, have all the strange resonance of a ceremony in white. In the film *Phantom Thread* (2017, dir. Paul Thomas Anderson), set in London in the 1950s, the designer enters the workroom, dressed immaculately in a suit rather than the T-shirt and trainers of today. He adjusts here and tweaks there, cutting a neck wider, a hem a little shorter, and stands back to envisage the white cotton in his mind's eye, in the right colour and weight of luxurious fabric. His job is to imagine, the sewers to bring those imaginings into being, and the model is an object in this context, her form waiting to be perfected in prototype.

We can be slaves to our memories, beset by images that we may never be able to understand fully and that may recur again and again, outside our conscious control. What influences our sartorial tastes is a mysterious business. These eerie toile-dressed models are ghostly figures, sometimes so abnormally slender and long-limbed that they resemble the distorted creatures of nightmares, like the dummies of artist Paula Rego come to life.

Backstage at the Royal Opera House in London, a friend once watched Rudolf Nureyev from the wings, then in the latter stages of his career, pirouetting on one spot, wearing white leotard and tights. It was very hot and still, and the knitted fabric was pulled tight, revealing the contours of his lean dancer's body beneath, the white becoming a transparent grey against his damp skin. The crew looked on sullenly it seemed, but then she became aware of a sort of swallowed panting, for they were counting '... three ... four ... five ...' willing him to keep going, as he turned on and on. As they did so, a spray of sweat would hit them, eight ... or was it ten ...? And then the audience erupted in applause. It is rare not to be disgusted by another's sweat, particularly a stranger's, but this had felt like an extraordinary privilege. Nureyev was apparently not best known for the excellence of his pirouettes, but he made a lasting impression of sheer determination that night. A ballerina's frothy tutu may come to mind when thinking of classical ballet, yet it is the male dancer here who diffused the whiteness of white.

It has been said that it is only dancers' bodies that can survive close scrutiny – that can look sleek rather than disappointing in

Edgar Degas, *Yellow Dancers (In the Wings)*, 1874–6, oil on canvas.

skin-tight white chamois trousers, say. The Italian prima ballerina Carla Fracci, who danced with Nureyev at La Scala, had a wardrobe that was almost entirely in shades of white, designed by her stylist Laura Biagiotti. One image shows her in a heavy silk dress that had once belonged to Eleonora Duse, looking like Klimt's Judith only without the gold; she is all in white, her hair piled around her face, languidly wearing the kimono-style gown. Fracci explained that she had first started dressing in white in 1969 during her pregnancy,[3] as if the associations of purity and innocence made her feel less vulnerable, her preference for smock-like silhouettes perhaps a reference to the nursery. Throughout her long life she continued to wear white, understanding that this adopted image was her way to be remembered, and that it came to stand for past glories in later life.

So many of our associations with clothing have been garnered from film and in this context have come to form our perception of white. The raw image of Renée Jeanne Falconetti in the silent film *The Passion of Joan of Arc* (1928, dir. Carl Theodor Dreyer) has Joan with shorn hair in a coarsely woven apparently undyed robe recanting her confession and facing the stake. Joan of Arc is represented in film and on stage in either a suit of silver armour or in a plain white tunic. For the test of her virginity Joan is usually depicted in white, as if to suggest by contrast the hymen's blood, as 'white clothing appears to be the preferred signifier of purity and chastity in cinematic representations of virginity.'[4]

In contrast, Marilyn Monroe's image, with her pleated white halter-neck dress flying up over the subway grating in *The Seven Year Itch* (1955), is all joyous, mischievous sensuality. Peter O'Toole in his flowing white Arab robes in *Lawrence of Arabia* (1962) is refined and beautiful, but the bumbling comic image of Fellini's soap-opera actor in *The White Sheik* (1952) is arguably just as memorable, a poor man's Rudolph Valentino perhaps, with Alberto Sordi enchanting a young bride. The terrifying figure of Tilda Swinton as the White Witch in *The Chronicles of Narnia* films competes with the superhuman figure of the Snow Queen in the Soviet animation of 1957 of that name; ice-bound female power is represented as a leitmotif in *Frozen* (2013). Mick Jagger gambols across the stage in his Mr Fish white frock in *Performance* (1968). This is only a small selection of the many films where white dress is used to create mood, various and eye-catching.

Ginger Rogers in *Top Hat* (1935) was determined to wear a gown by her favourite designer at the time, Bernard Newman. The dress was for a dance number with Fred Astaire, who, as soon as he saw it, took violently against the garment. The director, Mark Sandrich, attempted to persuade Rogers on Astaire's behalf that the satin and ostrich feather dress was unsuitable, but she refused outright to wear anything else. The dress was expensive and had required a specialist artisan to make it, costing in all about $1,500 at the time.[5] As they danced, filaments of the feathers began to detach themselves and, if you look carefully, you can see strands sticking to his black tail suit. He complained later that 'feathers started to fly as if a chicken had been attacked by a coyote . . . I never saw so many feathers in my life. It was like a snowstorm. They were floating around like millions of moths.'[6] Astaire opposed the dress before it had even begun to shed, so perhaps it was the attention-grabbing excess of the feathers that troubled him most. Since it was filmed in black and white, it is surprising to discover that the dress was in fact pale blue, and not white at all – and yet so it seems, dazzling, pure white.

White feathers can have a variety of meanings. They were a long-established symbol of cowardice in Britain, stemming from the adage that a fighting bird with white feathers in its tail was of inferior breeding, and women were encouraged to 'feather', that is, to shame, by giving a white chicken feather to non-uniformed men of apparent fighting fitness during the First World War. The idea of swaggering panache is derived from the white plumes worn on the hats of Italian Alpini officers. During the 1960s they were worn by American troops in Vietnam, as a taunt to enemy snipers. Contrarily, white feathers have been used as a pacifist emblem. Feathers have been used in fashion since antiquity, eighteenth-century headgear often relying on a vast, curling feather for its verve.[7] The Paris *plumassiers* of the seventeenth and eighteenth centuries had their own guild, with fifteen apprentices training for six years before they reached an acceptable standard. Feathers taken from living birds were more highly valued, but all required extensive preparation: 'White feathers could be bleached to obtain an even colour . . . White could be enhanced in baths of fine Spanish clay, or feathers could be exposed to sulphur fumes, much like wool.'[8]

The Bright Young Things of the post-First World War era wore trailing feather boas around their necks, signifying their exuberance. Coco Chanel had started out as a milliner in pre-war Paris, though her creations were far simpler than the fanciful, sometimes whole-bird, designs of the time, with often no more than a single ostrich feather dressing a plain straw hat. She ridiculed women at the races

Marilyn Monroe in *The Seven Year Itch* (1955, dir. Billy Wilder) with her pleated white halter-neck dress flying up over the subway grating.

Marlon Brando in a grubby white vest as Stanley Kowalski
in *A Streetcar Named Desire* (1951, dir. Elia Kazan).

for 'wearing enormous pies on their heads, monuments made of
feathers'.[9] In contrast, Dior delights in describing the exuberance of
lavish feather-themed balls such as one in 1937, where they danced
'in the ospreys and furbelows of Schiaparelli, on top of a grumbling
volcano'. He praises a colourful dance given by Charles de Beistegui
at his Venetian palace, exclaiming: 'The magic of a summer's night
in Italy held us in its eternal spell and put us outside time'.[10] And yet,
as far as Dior's own designs are concerned, a neutral palette seems to
dominate. In this respect, it is very like Chanel's.

In modern times white is with us all, providing wardrobe staples such as white T-shirts and trainers, those with fashion knowhow judging which items possess the coolest, most of-the-moment chic. The sleeveless white jersey undershirt was known as the 'dago-tee' in America in the 1900s, a derogatory term associating it with working-class Italian immigrants. Mid-century it became known as a 'wife beater', after a front-page news story about a Detroit man who was accused of beating his wife to death. He was pictured wearing a stained white undershirt beneath the caption, 'The Wife Beater'. Ever since Marlon Brando's sexually charged portrayal of Stanley Kowalski in *A Streetcar Named Desire* (1951, dir. Elia Kazan), there have been few would-be heartthrobs who have not had publicity shots taken in a plain white cotton jersey T-shirt, hoping to steal some of his pent-up machismo. They can be worn tight and revealing, or loose and grungy – or sometimes, as in the case of President John F. Kennedy, clean and correctly fitted, perfect for an ordinary man of the people. The white T has become a powerful image of casual style. Today the 1980s vintage white leather trainer has become desirable again, but the canny purchase of Primark or Tesco's F&F copies can create their own following, authentic becoming retro becoming an indicator of fashion nous, recalling one of Elsa Schiaparelli's Twelve Commandments for women's dress: 'She should buy little and only of the best or the cheapest.'[11] A designer knock-off is considered in a different light from one that does not pretend to be anything but cheap, even though 'the more minimal a clothing item is, the more its flaws become glaringly clear.'[12] The cognoscenti may recognize at a glance the most on-trend designer T-shirts and judge for themselves whether a faded Fruit of the Loom job is in fact more stylish than a stiff, new and expensive Michael Kors bearing his initials in crystals. A brand-new white pair of cotton-rich Marks & Spencer underpants are all fine and dandy but may fall short for the ultra-style conscious; better to be astonishingly cheap or worn thin with age, say some, than seem too safely middle-of-the-road.

The image of Robert Redford playing a has-been rodeo champion cowboy in the film *The Electric Horseman* (1979) has him kitted out in a suit blazing with tiny electric bulbs while promoting breakfast cereal. The suit's creator, Nudie Cohn, spent his childhood in Kiev, and became entranced by the Western films he was able to see at his local cinema. When he emigrated to the States, he began to tailor highly theatrical cowboy-style suits which came to be worn by some of the biggest names in country music and Hollywood. He put John Wayne in pale buckskin and Gram Parsons in white denim with a sparkling red cross on the back. Roy Rogers owned a huge collection of his suits, but perhaps most notable are the white leather cut-off jackets and sassy fringed skirts worn by Emmylou Harris and Dolly Parton. I recall Suzi Quatro in the television series *Happy Days* as Leather Tuscadero, lead singer of an all-female rock group, splendid in a Nudie white jumpsuit studded with rhinestones.

More recently Black rap artists have adopted all-white clothing, often in the gangster style, with oversized hoodies and high-top trainers, and all is blatantly brand new. Sean Combs quips, 'I feel safe in white, because deep down inside, I'm an angel.'[13] Biggie Smalls, also known as the Notorious B.I.G., often performed in a white suit, tie and bowler hat; Al Green regularly appears in white, in a reference to both Elvis and Nudie's designs. Kanye West wears white leggings and simple white T-shirts, giving almost the impression of a yoga guru, but then he also favours slick white suits with a black shirt beneath and large gold jewellery, a version of John Travolta in *Saturday Night Fever* perhaps. Dark skin and good teeth are offset by the bright white fabric.

A rather less flattering and well-worn white suit, donned by the British journalist turned MP Martin Bell, was claimed by him to have brought good luck when he was reporting in conflict zones. He became known as 'the man in the white suit', his clothing ill-fitting and definitely past its best, and yet it became a distinctive way of attracting publicity. When he required extensive facial surgery in 2019 after a fall, he was asked whether his suit was all that lucky after all, to which he insisted, 'I still have faith in it, absolutely. I'm sure without the suit it would have been much worse.'[14]

In the field of high fashion, where white continues to hold high office, there is always the undercurrent of fashion denigration to be faced. In many spheres the fact that luxurious white clothing catches the eye, can look splendid and suits the most stylish and beautiful people is not enough, or rather suggests too much self-absorption, vanity, self-love. In Shakespeare's *Much Ado About Nothing* Borachio dismisses fashion for being like a dishonest person:

> Seest thou not, I say, what a deformed thief this fashion is,
> How giddily he turns about all the hot bloods between
> Fourteen and thirty-five sometimes fashioning them
> Like Pharaoh's soldiers in the reechy painting, sometime
> Like god Bel's priests in the old church-window, sometime
> Like the shaven Hercules in the smirched worm-eaten
> Tapestry, where his codpieces seems as massy as his club?
> (iii.3)

He suggests that fashion in general – as in the *multum in parvo* of white clothing – has us aping uniforms, religious habits and heroes of the distant past, making us look foolish. But then this is a disgruntled character speaking, trying to persuade a friend, and even he admits that the argument is spurious. Fashion is necessarily about appearance, so that in that strict sense it is superficial. It is constantly changing, which is sometimes interpreted as a morally dubious characteristic. In most religions what is inner, and constant, is seen as of greater consequence, and yet we are essentially creatures of change. Clothing is something most of us have some control over, allowing us to express belonging or alternatively independence of mind and perhaps of taste. One question here is whether, in making choices about what we wear, there is a communication between maker and wearer. Some designers see themselves as artists set apart from the people who don their designs, whereas Chanel insisted that her work was a commercial exchange:

> A dress is neither a tragedy, nor a painting. It is a charming
> and ephemeral creation, not an everlasting work of art.
> Fashion should die and die quickly, in order that commerce
> may survive.[15]

This is, perhaps, a sensible position to hold, requiring less defence against a world where clothing can so often be seen as a form of empty egotism, as lacking the moral fibre of constancy. The curator Madeleine Delpierre, discussing eighteenth-century French dress, refers to Montesquieu's view of the flux of fashion: 'A woman who leaves Paris to spend six months in the country comes back as out of date as if she had been buried there for thirty years.'[16]

Such distinctions can rest on relatively small aspects of dress. In relation to accessories such as shoes and handbags, for example, white has on occasion been seen as a contentious, class-ridden attribute. In the days of disco, it was considered coarse when women who boogied in packs, with handbags at their feet for safekeeping, did so in matching cheap and shiny white patent stilettos. Patent shoes are potentially trashy since they are said to invite a glimpse of knicker, although Chanel herself habitually wore white patent shoes, along with the ropes of the 'defiantly fake' pearls she favoured.[17] In men's footwear white had long been associated with sportswear, white leather or leather-backed linen worn for golf, bowls and cricket. Today the white trainer has, to a great extent, taken over, so that even in the hallowed boutiques of Jermyn Street the finer points of what shoes should be worn when and where have largely been overthrown. A white suit is apparently rarely sought now, even the rich preferring the ease of separates, albeit with the right label.

The white brogue spectator shoe, with its main body in white or cream and the heel and toe cap in a darker colour, was first designed in 1868 by John Lobb for cricket, initially to keep grass stains from shoes, but they rapidly became the height of fashion in the late nineteenth century. It was in the post-First World War period that spectator shoes became associated with madcap behaviour, the Charleston dance craze and, by extension, immorality. They were also known as 'co-respondent' shoes, taken from the legal term for someone who acts as a third party in divorce cases, the person who is caught *in flagrante delicto* with the guilty married party, in order to prove their adultery. The elegant Wallis Simpson was known for wearing the particoloured shoes, though she was herself the guilty party, being a married woman: strictly speaking, it was Edward VIII who was the co-respondent.

In the early 1970s it was still considered by some arbiters of taste that, while it was acceptable for young girls to wear white ankle socks in cotton (never nylon), calf-length socks were associated with vulgarity and the lower classes. If calf-length socks were worn, they had to be made of fawn wool, or so I was schooled. In Japan in the 1980s, and still today in anime and in manga magazines, loose-fitting white calf-length socks on young teenagers are considered cute, often trimmed with lace, and particularly fetching if they happen to fall down unevenly, as if the wearer were too young and sweetly inept to be able to pull them up herself.

The Suffragette movement had embraced the trend for aesthetic white dresses in the 1880s and made it their own, 'countering and complicating the Edwardian taste for white'.[18] It was one of the three official suffrage colours, but purple and green tended to be accents to primary white in clothing, worn as contrasting sashes and cockades. The suffragists were mocked in the press for being frumpy, so that their hierarchy was keen to impose higher sartorial standards, and white suggested the right sort of spiritual and moral values. Because white is difficult to look after it also suggested that these women had social standing and were thus worthy of public respect. Sylvia Pankhurst rejoiced in the impression they made *en masse* in the United Procession of Women march for women's voting rights in February 1907, most of them dressed in white. Suffragists' more fashionable style of dress is described in an article in *Votes for Women* in 1908:

> The suffragette of today is dainty and precise in her dress;
> indeed, she has a feeling that, for the honour of the cause
> she represents, she must 'live up to' her highest ideals in all
> respects. Dress with her, therefore, is at all times a matter of
> importance, whether she is to appear on the public platform,
> in a procession, or merely in house or street about her
> ordinary vocations.[19]

The 'Living Pictures' series performed at St George's Hall in 1896 and conceived by the artist Walter Crane had, in one example, live suffragists posed like the classical Three Graces, dressed in white cotton frocks. In the Women's Coronation Procession of 1911, large numbers of suffragists marched, including those who had been imprisoned for their beliefs and were seen by many as martyrs to the cause, written of here in almost biblical terms:

> The most significant and beautiful part of the pageant was the contingent of those who had been in prison. They marched in white, a thousand strong, each one carrying a small silver pennant, and in their midst was borne a great banner depicting a symbolic woman with a broken chain in her hands and the inscription:
> FROM PRISON . . . TO CITIZENSHIP.[20]

White clothing has more recently been taken up by American congresswomen to express female solidarity, with the youngest in history, Alexandria Ocasio-Cortez, wearing a white trouser suit for her inauguration.[21] Shirley Chisholm wore white for her first day in Congress and also three years later, in 1972, when she announced her bid for the presidency. Geraldine Ferraro was in pearls and a white suit to accept her nomination as vice-president in 1984. Hillary Clinton wore white not only during her presidential campaign, but later when she attended the inauguration of Donald Trump. Jacqueline Kennedy wrote to Diana Vreeland that she considered white 'the most ceremonial colour', choosing it for both of her inaugural gowns for maximum visual impact.[22] She wore white more than any other shade on formal occasions, sometimes giving the impression of a bride among the more colourfully or darkly dressed. These First Lady gowns are often without embellishment: a cream woollen cape, a Chanel tweed coat, a plain shantung shift. More casually she is pictured again and again in white, getting off a plane or on holiday in Italy, in simple white shirt and slimline trousers, together with her trademark dark glasses.

White can seem the height of femininity in dress, daintily frilled or plain and simple, both associated with childhood and with naivety, whether knowing or sincere. Natalie Wood as Maria in the 1961 film version of *West Side Story* complains, 'White is for babies!' when shown the too-prim white-on-white embroidered cotton dress her cousin wants her to wear to a dance, and yet she changes her mind as soon as she tries it on.

The femininity of white: Berthe Morisot, *Woman at Her Toilette*,
1875–80, oil on canvas.

White dresses can also suggest a deceiving childishness, as in *The Great Gatsby*, where 'Daisy and Jordan lay upon an enormous couch, like silver idols weighing down their own white dresses against the singing breeze of the fans.'[23] These are women of means, and Daisy in particular plays upon her apparent fragility, epitomized by white dress, in order to be treated as needing male protection. Presenting themselves as idols suggests a desire for adoration. They are described as being 'bouyed up as though upon an anchored balloon', so carefree and, in this sense, light. Yet the contrast between the lightness of the breeze in their dresses and their intrinsic silver heaviness 'weighing down' implies their hidden intent.

Tailored white, on the other hand, can suggest women who want to be seen as in control. Sharon Stone in the film *Basic Instinct* (1992, dir. Paul Verhoeven) attracts attention in her dazzling white outfit, which draws our gaze to her shining, bronzed legs and beyond.

Women aspiring to power have to keep their whites spotless but also smart and sleek, any element of flounce resulting in them being taken less seriously. Men generally do business in dark suits as do women, but when the latter wear white they are making a statement, expressing their ethical purity.

Coco Chanel represents a pragmatic view of fashion and boasted that she had never bothered to learn how to ply a needle because she preferred to leave all that to skilled craftspeople. This is surprising, disingenuous even, since she had been taught to sew as a child in the orphanage of the abbey Aubazine in Corrèze, hemming sheets on Sundays, and later she was apprenticed to a local draper. It is said that her love of white and black stems from her memories of the white walls and tall black doors of the abbey. Christian Dior was more openly hands-on himself, but he greatly admired the skill and professionalism of his second-in-command, Madame Marguerite, claiming, 'She will stitch, unstitch, cut, cut again, a hundred times.'[24]

Photographs of Dior working on toiles in his studio comprise some of the most entrancing images of Parisienne *haute couture*. The simplicity of the toiles gives us a better, clearer understanding of his aims: 'the toiles have a little detail; their importance is entirely in their cut, line and shape. These are the fundamental toiles on which the whole collection is based.'[25]

In relation to this enquiry, Dior makes a telling general point about the role of white in his, and indeed any, collection, models wearing lighter fabrics he suggests being more arresting but also less commercial:

> dark and light dresses have to alternate wherever possible –
> although the light dresses are generally less numerous;
> the models which we guess will sell in large numbers,
> must be judiciously arranged and alternated with the
> spectacular models.[26]

A ballgown and train in heavily jewelled satin or a fairy-tale tulle wedding dress exquisitely hand-embroidered are important in the panoply of a great designer, but as in stage lighting, all the colours of the rainbow combine to focus in on one colourless colour, the fine details of design secondary to the governing concept. In the dramatic chiaroscuro of the catwalk, white is what sings. At the same time, on the eve of a collection, Dior describes his messengers rushing to and fro: 'Boys in white overalls scurry by, with tape measures round their necks.'[27] White clothing here is both exquisite fashion moment and everyday practical working uniform.

Charles Frederick Worth was the first designer to use live models for his Paris couturier in the 1850s. Before there were fashion models, dolls known as pandoras were used. Since the Middle Ages fashion dolls have worn miniature versions of adult clothing. They are not toiles or simplified versions, but made exactingly on a small scale, the workmanship and quality of fabrics far too precious to be a child's plaything. Catherine de Medici owned eight such fashion dolls

Pandora fashion doll *à la française*, c. 1760.

'dressed in elaborate mourning garb', purchased just after the death of her husband, as if they personified her grief.[28] The dressmaker Rose Bertin brought such doll models to Marie Antoinette for her appraisal. They involved a great deal of skilled labour, made more so by sewing on such a scale, the ladies of the court entranced by the lure of the miniature. There is some parity between smallness and whiteness, both intensifying our experience, taking us into the realm of the interior and of the concentrated imagination.

White is often considered to be difficult to carry off, exposing an imperfect figure and betraying any lurking lack of self-confidence. It may make for a dramatic silhouette, but many prefer not to take the risk. In an experiment to see how women's judgement is affected by perceptions of size in different coloured clothing, participants were shown a range of computer-generated models and asked to estimate their relative sizes. Unsurprisingly perhaps, white consistently achieved the most overestimated size readings.[29] White, then, does not flatter an imperfect figure and can even exaggerate our imperfections, yet at the same time it provides the greatest display for those who can carry it off. It promotes a fashion collection, even though it is the other colours that sell more. White is a supremely contradictory tradition and trope.

EIGHT

Whiteout

Let me be dress'd fine as I will,
Flies, worms, and flowers, exceed me still.
Isaac Watts (1674–1748), 'Against Pride in Clothes'

The novelist Benjamin Black's pathologist Quirke, in the Dublin of the 1950s, stumbles against a trolley carrying the shrouded body of a young woman and grabs the sheet to right himself, 'which came away in his hand in a hissing white flash. He was struck by the clammy coldness of the nylon; it had a human feel, like a loose, chill cowl of bloodless skin.'[1]

The funeral director's pall or more likely nowadays the zippered white plastic bag may turn out to be our final clothing. Morgues and winding sheets are the stuff of nightmares at times, but we are frequently drawn to their fearful domain. Shrouds cover coffins as well as wrap corpses, though clean, white sheets are also associated with sleep and sex and maybe even with the feeling of being safely tucked up in bed as a child.

In Christianity, the Shroud of Turin is believed by some to be the linen cloth in which Jesus of Nazareth was wrapped for burial, and which bears his image after his crucifixion:

As soon as he was dead, this Joseph of Arimathea who was a rich man went to Pilate, and begged the Body of Jesus; then

Pilate commanded the body to be delivered to him, and when Joseph had taken the body he wrapped it up in a clean Linen Cloth, and laid it in the Rock. (Matthew 27:58–60)

There has been much argument about the authenticity or otherwise of this winding cloth. Of the many accounts, the Gospel of Nicodemus, printed in 1507, identifies the daughter of a Lady Syndonya, the maid Syndonya, as the weaver of the cloth: 'I have wroughte the curyousest cloth that ever was made for it fyll gracyously to wourke that it is wore curious than I can skylle of.' Joseph of Arimathea is said to have referred to the shroud as the Syndonia.[2] The consensus now is that the shroud often identified as that of Jesus dates from the Middle Ages, though in 2013 Pope Francis said that it was still important as an 'icon of a man scourged and crucified'.

Linen cloth was used to wrap mummies in ancient Egypt from around 2600 BCE, during the fourth and fifth dynasties, and continued into 1075 BCE.[3] After the organs were removed and stored, only the heart was left in place, since it was considered the essential constituent of a person's spirit and intellect. The parts of the body that appear sunken after death were filled out with linen pads, treated and embalmed, with the facial features in particular carefully shored up. Priests used hundreds of metres of linen for a single body, wrapping every finger and toe separately, the whole process taking about seventy days of intensive labour. Recent scholarship suggests that the Egyptians were not so much obsessed with death but rather that they wanted to extend the pleasures of life, for which the body had to be kept intact. Embalming was so expensive a process that it was largely only the pharaohs and nobility who were mummified, though some animals were also embalmed for religious reasons. For all that were treated, the wrappings were of white linen.

In the modern day, mummies have become objects of terror in popular horror fiction and film. The curse of the pharaoh would fall on anyone, thief or archaeologist, who broke the seal of a tomb, and dared to unwrap an embalmed body. This superstition has been dated to the opening of Tutankhamun's tomb in the Valley of the Kings in Luxor in 1922, after the financer of the enterprise, Lord Carnarvon, died from blood poisoning only six weeks later. However, others insist that the idea of a curse had been around since the pyramids were first built, drawing on evidence found in certain hieroglyphics, and suggest it may have been intended as a deterrent against grave-robbing. Dominic Montserrat argues that it may have been a stage show in the mid-nineteenth century, in which real mummies were unwrapped in a bizarre form of striptease, that brought about the modern belief in the pharaoh's curse.[4] Whatever its origins, the image of the vengeful mummy, trailing its filthy bandages and emanating malevolence, has appeared in many subsequent films, the mummies of the British Museum attracting an audience unlike any other in its cathedral-like halls.

White was one of the mourning colours of ancient Rome because of 'its absence of positive colour and association with purity'.[5] In Hinduism, white is still widely adopted to express grief and widowhood. It was worn for the first and deepest mourning period of medieval European queens, and in the sixteenth century Mary, Queen of Scots, was seen *en deuil blanc*, white mourning, for an extended period after losing three close relatives in the period from 1559 to 1561: her father-in-law, Henry II of France, her mother, Mary of Guise, and her husband, Francis II. She was depicted in a graceful Paris or French cap by François Clouet in about 1660–61 on her return to Scotland, in an image that was much copied and circulated throughout the courts of Europe. Her headdress, an attifet made of white linen, was also worn by Catherine de Medici but became known as a Mary Stuart cap. In Clouet's painting it has a triangle of stiffened fabric edged with pearls which dips down in the centre of the forehead to create a heart shape when viewed from the front. A white veil is arranged over the cap, with Mary's hair clustered on each temple. On her chin she wears a finely pleated white linen *barbe* or extended wimple, attached on either side to the veil. She was renowned for her beauty, an observer commenting on: 'the whiteness of her face [which] rivalled the whiteness of her veils, and in this context artifice was the loser, the veils paling before the snows of her skin'.[6]

The cap design was already two centuries out of date but was still worn by some religious orders. When it became fashionable again in

François Clouet, *Mary, Queen of Scots*, c. 1560–61, oil on panel.

the late sixteenth century in England, there were rules concerning how high or low on the forehead the cap should be worn, relating to rank.[7] In such fine distinctions of clothing is status best expressed.

Since the early Christian Church, widows had sometimes retired to a convent and adopted the habit and veil to lead a simple life apart. Indeed, the pale tomb effigies of departed kings and queens in our great cathedrals, and even more modest memorials in church and chapel, add to this sombre impression of white and its relation to death. An example in the film *Robin and Marian* (1976, dir. Richard Lester) has Audrey Hepburn's Maid Marian not only retiring to a convent but becoming an abbess and wearing a plain white habit of office. She is rescued against her will from the Sheriff of Nottingham's men by an ageing Robin Hood, played by Sean Connery. The two end up united in death, like an aged Romeo and Juliet, she in her nun's robes and he in bandages and a white undershirt.

In some regions of France young women were buried in white and with orange-blossom wreaths well into the twentieth century. In southern Germany a Death Wedding ceremony dressed deceased young people in white to suggest the virgin bride or groom were going to their spiritual marriage in death. They wore tall white crowns, sometimes initialled 'J' for *Jungfrau*, or virgin.[8] In the many stages of dark mourning practised throughout Europe by those who could afford it, white crêpe remained the final stage. However, in Angela Thirkell's novel *The Brandons* (1939) the elderly Aunt Sissie has been wearing black for many years 'what with one death and another'. She assumes that Mrs Brandon, widowed for only four months, must be pregnant, for she can imagine no other possible reason to be dressed in white so soon: 'Her gaze was again so meaningly fixed upon her niece's white dress that Mrs Brandon began to blush violently.'[9] Mrs Brandon rallies, claiming that it was 'less depressing for the children', and no doubt for her. White might have been, in Aunt Sissie's day, a final stage of mourning but, as with Queen Victoria, it could be a very long and drawn-out business getting there.

Traditional Russian funeral practice has the deceased clothed in white and in Orthodox funeral rites the priest wears white vestments. In folk culture the white robes of the corpse are left unhemmed and unfinished, as a sign that they belong to the world of their ancestors. The Imperial Court ordained that, in the later stages of mourning, women were to wear white silk crêpe, or white woollen fabric decorated with crêpe. However, the same white clothing could be adopted, even by those of great status, for very different occasions. An example of this is the dress worn for the funeral of Emperor Alexander III in 1894 by his widow, Maria Feodorovna, which she went on to wear for the wedding of her son Nicholas II less than one month later.[10]

In indigenous Australian culture, widows wear caps, or *kopis*, made of weighty white plaster, sometimes for up to six months. The thicker and heavier they are, the deeper the grief is said to be.[11] It is customary in Muslim funerals to wrap the deceased in white cloth. Yorubans wear white to mediate with their ancestor spirits.[12] In Cambodia, where Buddhism is the official religion, when somebody dies white is the traditional colour for funerals and mourning. It is also worn for the body's cremation.

Chinese tradition has mourners in a variety of either undyed hemp, white linen or muslin clothing, obeying strictly defined categories depending on the relationship to the deceased.[13] During the early twentieth century professional mourners in China wore white clothing, their role being to school the bereaved in how they should behave and what clothing they should adopt. Close relatives had to abide by the complex rules for as long as 27 months. This could be problematic for those in important positions, since the restrictions could distract them from the business of staying in power. However, if they were seen to ignore the rules then they could be thought of as indifferent to and disrespectful of their ancestors.

Japanese emperors wore white silk robes, the *byakue*, which were then adopted by Shinto priests, with Buddhist priests wearing more commonplace hemp. Japanese ghosts, the *yūrei*, are depicted with long black hair, white faces and white garments. Thus three categories of people are associated with white clothing: royalty, priests and the living dead. It remains traditional in both native Shinto and Buddhist custom to be buried in a white kimono. Shintoism holds that white represents purity, and in Buddhism white dress is worn by the dead and the dying, including those preparing for death, as in the custom of *seppuku*. All are in white at the outset of their journey beyond death, their colourless clothing representing the relinquishing of all earthly desires. This dress of the dead is a ritual more defined than a Western trousseau, consisting of the *kyōkatabira*, a gown with sutras written on the inside, the *tenkan*, a triangular headdress, various coverings for the arms, legs and back, and a small bag, the *zutabukuro*, for the ferry crossing over the Sanzu river of the dead – all in pristine white cotton cloth. Whereas the kimono is usually worn with the left

Eugène Delacroix, *Marguerite's Ghost Appearing to Faust*, c. 1828, lithograph.

side overlapping the right because it is said to allow greater freedom of movement, the *katabira* of the dead is worn right over left. Zack Davisson refers to the shock, sometimes amusement, caused when foreigners put on a kimono right over left, unwittingly associating themselves with the dead.[14] Historically, an aristocrat would have been dressed by a servant and thus the normal left-to-right practice would be reversed, the difference coming to represent high status and only more recently with dressing the dead.[15]

Experience of phantoms is usually held to occur at night, so it is unsurprising that what is reported tends to seem pale in the darkness. Often the spectral world is whitened, with white clouds, white miasma, smoke and pale ghostly effluvia, and of course the spirits are clothed in white, or we would not be able to see them. Ghostly figures are insubstantial, it seems, and they are frequently described as wearing flowing robes or trailing, tattered shrouds. It was not until the seventeenth century in Europe that people other than the nobility would have hoped to be buried in a coffin rather than being wrapped in a shroud alone, so it is perhaps unsurprising that wandering ghosts came to be envisaged in their winding cloths, of plain undyed linen or wool.

The white lady legend is found in many versions across the world and her appearance augurs death. She represents tragic loss and betrayal. In the Netherlands, for instance, a woman who was reputedly burnt to death on her wedding day is said to wander the Schinveldse Bossen forest in a long white dress by the light of a full moon, that symbol of change and infidelity.

In 1804 a man was found guilty of murder for shooting what he believed to be a ghost. There had been many reports of a spectre being at large, terrifying the inhabitants of Hammersmith, West London, and causing the untimely deaths of several nervous women. Francis Smith, a member of an armed patrol set up to protect citizens from this threat, felt justified in killing the malevolent being. He warned it, it failed to stop and so he shot it dead. Sadly, it had turned out to be only a bricklayer, one Thomas Millwood, returning late from work in the white uniform of his trade, which included 'linen trousers, entirely white, washed very clean, a waistcoat of flannel, apparently new, very white, and an apron, which he wore round him'.[16] Smith was found guilty of murder and the case set a legal precedent that was not repealed until 1984. It turns out that the original hoaxer, and source of the panic, had been an elderly shoemaker who had felt his apprentice needed to be taught a lesson, and had dressed in ghostly white garb to shock him into better behaviour.

The wandering dead are often depicted as retaining the frailties and idiosyncrasies of the living. How else could anyone imagine them but as essentially human? Such familiarity might also be said to make death itself appear less alarming. In the 1969–70 television detective drama *Randall and Hopkirk (Deceased)* both characters, the living and the dead, are equally human and fallible. Hopkirk is dressed in glowing, sometimes semi-transparent white and is only visible to one other, in this case Randall, a common conceit of ghost stories.

Similarly, in *A Chinese Fairy Tale*, a fantasy film of 2011 from Wilson Yip, the visibility of the ghost is limited.[17] In both, the ghostly figure is dressed in white and their motives are hidden, and we discover that their hauntings are mainly concerned with putting right wrongs done to them when they were alive, the white garb suggesting that their objectives are justified rather than malevolent.

Just as swaddling bands protected the newborn child, there is, in the collection of the Victoria and Albert Museum, a small burial shirt, 'made of a single piece of uncomplicated, uncoloured cloth'. Now grimy with age, it dates from the fifth or sixth century, when once 'it would have cleanly enshrined the deceased, a final formality for the person'.[18] Yet this shift has been intricately embroidered, as if there had been some expression of grief in its making, weaving into its fabric something of the life that had been so briefly lived: 'Motifs, circular patterns, spiralling vines and abstract shapes, while tiny heads, flowers, birds and animals come together to add a delicate sense of personality to the fabric and the wearer.'

The white sheet or shroud is associated not only with death but with sleep and with sexual intimacy, and thus with safe rest and with desire and even dangerous passion. In *The Winter's Tale* the sheets for Leontes represent betrayal, his wife and friend sullying 'the purity and whiteness of my sheets' (1.2).

The poet John Donne (1572–1631) put on his shroud while gravely ill, obsessed with preparations for his death and planning how he should be remembered:

> Several Charcoale-fires being first made in his large study, he brought with him into that place his winding-sheet in his hand, and having put off all his clothes, had his sheet put upon him, and so tied with knots at his head and feet, and his hands so placed as dead bodies are usually fitted to be shrouded and put in the grave. Upon [the] Urn he thus stood with his eyes shut, and so much of the sheet turned aside as might show his lean, pale, and death-like face, which was purposely turned towards the East, from whence he expected the second coming of our Saviour ... when the picture was finished, he caused it

to be set by his bed-side . . . and became his hourly object till his death.[19]

Nicholas Stone was to sculpt his statue in white marble after Donne's death, based on this sketch. It now stands in the new St Paul's Cathedral, one of the few monuments to have survived the Great Fire of London in 1666, its whiteness scorched at its base.

Queen Victoria was keen on funerals. She enjoyed discussing with her ladies-in-waiting the details of coffins and winding sheets and she even held burials for her beloved dogs. After years of wearing black following Prince Albert's death, she planned a white funeral for herself. She was to be dressed in white, and in her coffin, along with various 'itemized rings, chains, bracelets, lockets, shawls, the Prince Consort's dressing gown which had been embroidered by Princess Alice and a plaster cast of his hand [and] numerous photographs', her wedding day white lace veil was to be laid over her face.[20] She had worn this veil to all her children's christenings and in her later years to all important family events. She insisted upon her daughters and daughters-in-law following her example by also wearing white Honiton lace wedding veils, partly to support the Devon lacemakers' trade, but also to oppose the more fashionable foreign Brussels lace.

Victoria's love of continuity and of white mourning appears to have caught on. In 1938, Queen Elizabeth the Queen Mother, on the sudden death of her mother, had to go into mourning on the eve of her departure for a state visit to Paris with her husband, King George VI. The wardrobe, by Norman Hartnell, therefore had to be hastily re-made, now all in white, a symbol of royal mourning recalling Queen Victoria's funeral 37 years before. Her appearance was admired by some, with journalist Georgina Howell enthusing:

> Elizabeth's filmy white dresses, combined with her blue eyes and perfect complexion, upstaged every couture dress in every room she entered, and when she appeared at a garden party at the Bagatelle, face framed against a white parasol, the train of her snowy lace dress trailing behind her across the grass, she won everyone's heart.[21]

Princess Diana and Prince Charles paid an official visit to the city of high fashion in 1988 and, as with Charles's grandmother, Diana's fashion choices were much discussed, in particular several white and black-and-white outfits. Unlike the Queen Mother, her style was tailored, with double-breasted coat dresses, one especially striking example being a plain black outfit with a glamorous white faux-fur deep-lapelled collar, which she wore for the opening of a branch of Marks & Spencer in central Paris.

A wedding day is linked to funeral rights, to religious dress and to the supernatural, which duly refers back again to high fashion, all through the medium of white dress, connecting with its qualities of purity, cleanliness and solemnity, but also at times to its sheer pazazz. This has been a reflection on white clothing and on the wearing of white, from blank white elegance to all the fuss of frilly furbelow, the liquefaction of dreams to the stuff of the everyday. There are garments that exist only in the mind, but also those of wool, cotton, linen and silk, that can remind us of the body beneath or the spirit of the person who once wore them. There are clothes we have never worn and have yet to wear, and there is the way what we wear becomes part of who we are.

Clothing matters and white clothing deserves special mention, for all its grand, subtle and most ordinary significance through time. And so, to return to Homer, this time via Mark Twain, who took to wearing white alone towards the end of his life: 'Clothes make the man. Naked people have little or no influence in society.'[22]

References

Introduction

1 For example, the Labor Day 'rule' in the USA, according to which, after the first Monday in September, white clothing should not be worn – except by those affluent enough to take autumn and winter holidays in sunnier climes.

2 Cited in Justine Picardie, *Coco Chanel: The Legend and the Life* (London, 2010), p. 200.

3 Ibid., p. 199.

4 J. C. Flügel, *The Psychology of Dress* (London, 1930).

5 Dipesh Chakrabarty, 'Clothing the Political Man: A Reading of the Use of Khadi/White in Indian Public Life', *Journal of Postcolonial Studies*, IV/1 (London, 2001), p. 28.

ONE The Ancient Gods of Fashion

1 Joan Allgrove-McDowell, 'Ancient Egypt, 5000–332 BC', in *The Cambridge History of Western Textiles*, ed. David Jenkins (Cambridge, 2003), vol. I, p. 37.

2 Plutarch, *Life of Antony*, 33.4.

3 Page Dubois, 'Popular Belief About the Human Body in Antiquity', in *A Cultural History of the Human Body in Antiquity*, ed. Daniel H. Garrison (Oxford, 2010), p. 108; Brooke A. Holmes, 'Marked Bodies (Gender, Race, Class, Age, Disability, Disease)', in *A Cultural History of the Human Body in Antiquity*, p. 171.

4 Maria Millington Evans, *Chapters on Greek Dress* [1893] (Ithaca, NY, 2009), p. 2.

5 Homer cited ibid., p. 9.

6 Ibid., p. 61.

7 Glenys Davies, 'What Made the Roman Toga *Virilis*', in *The Clothed Body in the Ancient World*, ed. Liza Cleland, Mary Harlow and Lloyd Llewellyn-Jones (Oxford, 2005), p. 127.

8 Alexandra Croom, *Roman Clothing and Fashion* (Stroud, 2011), p. 110.

9 Evans, *Greek Dress*, p. 52.

10 Quoted in Kelly Olson, *Masculinity and Dress in Roman Antiquity* (London, 2017), p. 124.

11 Ibid.

12 Alan Sinfield, *The Wilde Century: Effeminacy, Oscar Wilde, and the Queer Moment* (New York, 1994), pp. 40–41.

13 Garments were woven by the lady of the house and her servants. Marina Fischer, 'Ancient Greek Prostitutes and the Textile Industry in Attic Vase-Painting, *c*. 550–450 BCE', *Classical World*, CVI/2 (Winter 2013), pp. 219–59, citing Homer's *Iliad*, book 3, line 388; *Odyssey*, book 18, line 316; and *Iliad*, book 22, on p. 511.

14 Ibid., p. 220.

15 Ibid., p. 222.

16 Evans, *Greek Dress*, p. 4.

17 Holmes, 'Marked Bodies', p. 174.

18 Ibid., p. 177.

19 *The Letters of Cicero*, trans. Evelyn S. Shuckburgh (London, 1899), vol. I, www.gutenberg.org, p. 68.

20 Olson, *Masculinity and Dress*, p. 81.

21 Ibid., p. 113.

22 Giovanni Fanfani, Mary Harlow and Marie-Louise Nosch, ed., *Spinning Fates and the Song of the Loom: The Use of Textiles, Clothing and Cloth Production as Metaphor, Symbol and Narrative Device in Greek and Latin Literature* (Oxford, 2016), p. 324.

23 Robert Sellers, *Don't Let the Bastards Grind You Down* (London, 2012), p. 358.

TWO The Spiritual, the Professional and the Uniform

1 Beverly Gordon, *Textiles: The Whole Story – Uses, Meanings, Significance* (London, 2011), p. 25.

2 One of the vesting prayers said when a Catholic priest puts on his white alb/tunic before mass. 'Why Do Priests Wear White Albs?', https://aleteia.org, 20 April 2017.

3   Comte de Buffon, *De L'homme* (Paris, 1771), cited in Denis Bruna,
    Fashioning the Body: An Intimate History of the Silhouette (New York,
    2015), p. 89.

4   Alison Lurie, *The Language of Clothes* (New York, 1981), p. 185.

5   According to the ancient Jewish scholar Flavius Josephus, cited in
    Eibert J. C. Tigchelaar, 'The White Dress of the Essenes and the
    Pythagoreans', in *Jerusalem, Alexandria, Rome: Studies in Ancient
    Cultural Interaction*, p. 301, in supplements to the *Journal for the Study
    of Judaism* (Leiden, 2003), vol. LXXXII.

6   Except in the case of martyred saints, where white vestments are
    considered too joyful, and red vestments are worn instead.

7   Gordon, *Textiles*, p. 256.

8   Gautier de Coinci (1177–1236), *Cinq Miracles de Notre-Dame*,
    ed. Jean-Louis Gabriel Benoit (Paris, 2007).

9   Fiona Maddocks, *Hildegard of Bingen: The Woman of Her Age*
    (London, 2001), pp. 1–2.

10 Janet Fairweather, *Liber Eliensis: A History of the Isle of Ely from
    the Seventh Century to the Twelfth Century, Compiled by a Monk
    of Ely in the Twelfth Century* (Woodbridge, 1995), pp. 187–8.

11 Muriel Spark, *The Abbess of Crewe* (London, 1974), p. 9.

12 Ibid., p. 1.

13 Cited in John Harvey, *Men in Black* (London, 1995), p. 205.

14 Cordelia Warr, 'Belief', in *The Cultural History of Dress and
    Fashion in the Renaissance*, ed. Elizabeth Currie (London, 2017),
    chap. 4.

15 'Without sins a soul is like a polished mirror or a white cloth':
    Prayers and Supplications of the Prophet, www.islamiccenter.org,
    accessed 14 November 2021.

16 Gordon, *Textiles*, p. 257.

17 Joanna Moorhead, 'The Wind in My Hair: One Woman's Struggle
    Against the Hijab', *The Observer*, 2 June 2018.

18 Elizabeth Bucar, *Pious Fashion: How Muslim Women Dress*
    (London, 2017), p. 169.

19 Nina Tarasova of the Costume Department at the State Hermitage
    Museum, St Petersburg, email to author, 5 October 2021.

20 Leo the Deacon, Byzantine historian, describes Prince Igorevich,
    military conqueror of 945–72 CE, as having a preference for wearing
    white, and being notably cleaner than his men, and was present at
    this meeting between the prince and John I Tzimisces.

21 David Nicolle, 'Armies of Medieval Russia, 750–1250', *Men at Arms*,
    333 (15 November 1999), p. 44.

22 Suzanne Lenglen was ranked the first world number one female tennis player, holding the position from 1921 to 1926.

23 Elizabeth Wilson, *Love Game: A History of Tennis, from Victorian Pastime to Global Phenomenon* (London, 2014), p. 42.

24 Ibid., p. 149.

25 Richard Evans, 'Gussie Moran', obituary, *The Guardian* (20 January 2013).

26 Lena Williams, 'Gussie Moran', obituary, *New York Times* (18 January 2013); 'In Memory of Gorgeous "Gussie" Moran', www.wimbledon.com, 30 January 2013.

27 Adam Augustyn, 'Why Do Tennis Players Wear White at Wimbledon?', www.britannica.com, accessed 16 November 2021.

28 Advertisement for Sipsmith, devised by Jules Chalkley of Ogilvy UK.

29 Kimberly A. Miller, *The Meanings of Dress*, 3rd edn (London, 2012), p. 269, citing Aileen Ribeiro, *Dress and Morality* (London, 1986).

30 Jamie Lynn Capparelli, 'Nursing Nuns', *American Journal of Nursing*, VIII/105 (August 2005), https://journals.lww.com.

31 Interview with Barbara Bradley Hagerty, American National Public Radio, 22 December 2010.

32 See, for instance, Hamidreza Rochafza et al., 'Impact of Nurses' Clothing on Anxiety of Hospitalized Children', *Journal of Clinical Nursing* (5 June 2009), a clinical study of seven- to fifteen-year-olds in Iran; Lauren Keblunek and Howard Giles, 'Dress Style Code and Fashion', www.oxford.research.encyclopedia, July 2017.

33 John Good, of No. 8 Dental Partnership, London, email to author, 24 June 2022.

34 Hajo Adam and Adam D. Galinsky, 'Enclothed Cognition', *Journal of Experimental Social Psychology* (19 January 2012).

35 It has been argued that professional sports teams who wear black uniforms are more aggressive than those wearing non-black. M. G. Frank and T. Gilovich, 'The Dark Side of Self- and Social Perception: Black Uniforms and Aggression in Professional Sports,' *Journal of Personality and Social Psychology*, XLIV/1 (1988), pp. 74–85.

36 Dino Felluga, 'Modules on Foucault: On Power', https://purdue.edu, 2021.

37 P. G. Wodehouse, *Right Ho Jeeves* (London, 1934), p. 17.

THREE Fashionable Men, Veils and Gloves

1 Margaret Scott, *Medieval Dress and Fashion* (London, 2007), p. 7.

2 Ibid., p. 131.

3 Bibles moralisées were thirteenth-century selections from the Bible, accompanied by commentaries and illustrations.

4 Mary G. Houston, *Medieval Costume in England and France: The 13th, 14th and 15th Centuries* [1939] (London, 1996), p. 98.

5 Jack Hartnell, *Medieval Bodies: Life, Death and Art in the Middle Ages* (London, 2018), p. 102.

6 'The Many Layers of Hanbok: Chima Jeogori', www.the krazemag.com, 28 July 2019.

7 Tatsuichi Horikiri, *The Stories Clothes Tell: Voices of Working-Class Japan*, ed. and trans. Rieka Wagoner (London, 2016), p. 135.

8 Scott, *Medieval Dress*, p. 144.

9 Denis Bruna, *Fashioning the Body: An Intimate History of the Silhouette* (New York, 2015), p. 31.

10 Ibid., p. 32.

11 Cennino Cennini, *Trattato della Pittura* (1821).

12 'History of Laundry', www.oldandinteresting.com, accessed 7 April 2021.

13 Werner Rösener, *Peasants in the Middle Ages*, trans. Alexander Stützer (Oxford, 1992), p. 86.

14 Anne van Buren, *Illuminating Fashion: Dress in the Art of Medieval France and Netherlands, 1325–1515* (London, 2011), p. 17.

15 Mary C. Erler, 'Margery Kempe's White Clothes', *Medium Ævum*, LXII/1 (1993), p. 79.

16 Cited in Guillemette Bolens and Sarah Brazil, 'The Life of Christina of Markyate', in *A Cultural History of Dress and Fashion in the Medieval Age*, ed. Sarah-Grace Heller (London, 2018), vol. II, p. 84.

17 The value attached to ermine was not only monetary but derived from the belief that it was a creature of such purity and honour that it would prefer to die rather than soil its fur. See also Margaret Scott, *Medieval Dress*, p. 145.

18 Chaucer's 'The Former Age', cited in John S. Lee, *The Medieval Clothier* (Belfast, 2018), p. 13.

19 Carole Rawcliffe, *Leprosy in Medieval England* (Woodbridge, 2006), p. 329.

20 Ibid., pp. 266, 289.

21 Hartnell, *Medieval Bodies*, p. 108.

22 John Nichols, ed., *The Progresses and Public Processions of Queen Elizabeth* (London, 1823), vol. II, p. xlii.

23 Hugo Falcandus referring to silk production in Italy in 1190, in *The History of the Tyrants of Sicily, 1154–1169*, quoted in Anna Muthesius,

'Silk in the Medieval World', in *The Cambridge History of Western Textiles*, ed. David Jenkins (Cambridge, 2003), vol. I, p. 331.

24 Joan Think, 'Knitting and Knitwear, *c.* 1500–1780', in *The Cambridge History of Western Textiles*, ed. Jenkins, vol. II, p. 573.

25 'William Lee', www.christs.cam.ac.uk, accessed 6 July 2022.

26 At www.oldandinteresting.com/laundry-blue, accessed 5 July 2022.

27 Ibid.

28 Amelia Chambers, *The Ladies Best Companion; or, A Golden Treasure for the Fair Sex* [1775] (London, 2010).

29 Bruna, *Fashioning the Body*, pp. 71 and 73.

30 Ibid., p. 21.

31 John Davies, 'Upon a Paire of Garters', in *The Complete Poems of Sir John Davies* (London, 1876), p. 224.

32 Bruna, *Fashioning the Body*, p. 32.

33 Thomas Kemp, ed., *The Black Book of Warwick* (Warwick, 1898), pp. xxvii–xxviii.

34 Annet Couwenberg, quoted in David Revere McFadden, *Radical Lace and Subversive Knitting* (New York, 2010), p. 13.

35 Ibid., p. 48.

36 Antoine de Baecque and Noël Herpe, *Éric Rohmer: A Biography* (New York, 2016), pp. 448–9.

37 William Shakespeare, *The Winter's Tale*, directed by Trevor Nunn and designed by Christopher Morley, with Barrie Ingham as Leontes and Judi Dench as both Hermione and Perdita, Royal Shakespeare Company, 1969–70.

38 In contrast, Leontes in *The Winter's Tale* thinks he finds evidence of Hermione's infidelity because she allows Polixenes to take her hand (1.3).

39 Susan Frye, 'The Myth of Elizabeth at Tilbury', *Sixteenth Century Journal*, XXIII/1 (Spring 1992), pp. 95–114.

40 Carolly Erickson, *The First Elizabeth* [1983] (New York, 1999), pp. 373–4.

41 Quentin Bell, *On Human Finery* (London, 1976), p. 29.

42 Fiona McCarthy, *Last Curtsey: The End of the Debutantes* (London, 2006), p. 85.

43 Ibid.

44 Michelle K. Gillespie and Catherine Clinton, eds, *Taking off the White Gloves: Southern Women and Women Historians* (Columbia, MO, 1998).

45 Louisa May Alcott, *Little Women* (Boston, MA, 1868), chap. 3.

FOUR Powdered Wigs and Muslins

1 Thorstein Veblen, *The Theory of the Leisure Class* [1899] (London, 1994), p. 109.
2 Gustave Flaubert, *Madame Bovary* [1856], trans. Geoffrey Wall (London, 1992), p. 37.
3 Ibid., p. 39.
4 Ibid., pp. 39–40 and 237.
5 James G. McLaren, 'A Brief History of Wigs in the Legal Profession', *International Journal of the Legal Profession*, VI/2 (1999).
6 James Laver, *Costume* (London, 1963), p. 70.
7 Michael Driscoll, 'Church Architecture and Liturgy in the Carolingian Era', in *A Companion to the Eucharist in the Middle Ages*, ed. Ian Levy et al. (London, 2011), p. 195. Louis also sent his unmarried sisters, half-sisters and nieces into convents, for fear of any threat from husbands they might otherwise obtain.
8 'The Rise and Fall of the Powdered Wig', www.battlefields.org, 26 May 2020.
9 Mary Frampton, *The Journal of Mary Frampton: From the Year 1779, until the Year 1846, including Various Interesting and Curious Letters, Anecdotes, etc., Relating to Events which Occurred During that Period* (London, 1885), pp. 2–3.
10 The diary of Samuel Pepys, 3 September 1665, www.pepysdiary.com.
11 'Women's Hairstyles and Cosmetics of the 18th Century', www.demode.couture.com, accessed 17 January 2021, citing Desmond Hosford, 'The Queen's Hair: Marie-Antoinette, Politics, and DNA', *Eighteenth Century Studies*, XXXVIII/1 (2004), pp. 183–200.
12 Oscar Wilde, *The Importance of Being Earnest* (London, 1895), Act I.
13 Madeleine Delpierre, *Dress in France in the Eighteenth Century* (London, 1998), p. 1.
14 James Laver suggests that when waists are in the wrong place, meaning not at the bodily waist, either high as in the 1750s or low as in the 1920s, it is a sign of a post-crisis period, which are 'never strait-laced, either physically or morally' (Laver, *Costume*, p. 77).
15 Caroline London, 'The Marie Antoinette Dress that Ignited the Slave Trade', www.racked.com, 10 January 2018.
16 Caroline Weber, *Queen of Fashion: What Marie Antoinette Wore to the Revolution* (New York, 2007), cited ibid.
17 Amelia Rauser, *The Age of Undress: Art, Fashion and the Classical Ideal in the 1790s* (London, 2020), p. 14.

18 William Hazlitt, 'On Fashion', *Edinburgh Magazine*, III (September 1818).

19 *The Oxford Magazine*, 1770, quoted in Joseph T. Shipley, *The Origins of English Words: A Discursive Dictionary of Indo-European Roots* (London, 1984), p. 143.

20 Nina Tarasova of the Costume Department at the State Hermitage Museum, St Petersburg, email to author, 5 October 2021.

21 Inna Fedorova, 'Dressing Like a Dictator: Stalin's Distinctive Military Chic', *Rossiyskaya Gazeta*, 20 August 2014, at www.rbth.com.

22 *Shocking Life: The Autobiography of Elsa Schiaparelli* (London, 2007), p. 85.

23 William Henry Ireland, *The Life of Napoleon Bonaparte* (London, 1828), vol. IV, pp. 531–2.

24 Ibid.

25 Ibid., p. 533.

26 Gail Marsh, *18th Century Embroidery Techniques* (Lewes, 2006), pp. 111–12.

27 Rozsika Parker, *The Subversive Stitch: Embroidery and the Making of the Feminine* [1984] (London, 2010), p. 139, citing Mary Wollstonecraft, *The Vindication of the Rights of Women* (1792).

28 Charlotte Brontë, *Jane Eyre* (London, 1847), chap. 10.

29 Gita May, 'A Courtly Salon on the Eve of the French Revolution: Élisabeth Louise Vigée Le Brun – Salonnière', in *Women Writers in Pre-Revolutionary France*, ed. Collette H. Winn and Donna Kulzenga (London, 1997).

30 Aileen Ribeiro, 'Muses, Mythology and Female Portraiture', in *Defining Dress: Dress as Object, Meaning and Identity*, ed. Amy de la Haye and Elizabeth Wilson (New York, 1999), p. 106.

31 Richard Cavendish, 'Emma Lady Hamilton Dies in Calais', *History Today*, LXV/1 (1 January 2015).

32 Aileen Ribeiro, 'Muses, Mythology', p. 106.

33 Thomas Gainsborough's *Mr and Mrs Andrews*, c. 1750, held at the National Gallery. The patch on Mrs Andrews's lap is thought to have been left unpainted so that a baby might be added in the future.

34 Jane Austen, *Northanger Abbey* (London, 1817), chap. 3.

35 Ibid.

36 Ibid., chaps 12 and 8.

37 Jane Austen, *Mansfield Park* (London, 1814), chap. 23.

38 Jane Austen, *Pride and Prejudice* (London, 1813), chap. 8.

39 Robert Herrick (1591–1614), 'Delight in Disorder'.

40 Thomas Hardy, *Tess of the d'Urbervilles* (London, 1891), chap. 11.

41 Aileen Ribeiro, 'Dress in the Early Modern Period', in *The Cambridge History of Western Textiles*, ed. David Jenkins (Cambridge, 2003), vol. I, p. 660.

42 Hazlitt, 'On Fashion'.

43 Charles Baudelaire, *Le Peintre de la Vie Moderne* [1860], trans. Jonathan Mayne (London, 1964), cited in Penelope Byrd, *The Male Image* (London, 1979) p. 17.

44 Wilkie Collins, *The Woman in White* (London, 1859), chap. 4.

45 Ibid., chap. 8.

46 Charles Dickens, *Great Expectations* (London, 1861), chap. 8.

47 Ibid., chap. 49.

48 Brontë, *Jane Eyre*, chap. 17.

49 Ibid., chap. 24.

50 Ibid., chap. 25.

51 Ibid.

52 Veblen, *Theory of the Leisure Class*, p. 103.

53 Captain William Jesse, *The Life of Beau Brummell* (London, 1844).

54 Grace and Philip Wharton, *Wits and Beaux of Society* (1861), cited at www.dandyism.net.

55 Brian Dillon, 'Inventory/A Poet of Cloth: Beau Brummell's Knot Theory', www.cabinetmagazine.com (Spring 2006); Dillon is quoting 'Neckclothitania or Tietania, Being an Essay on Starchers', written by 'one of the cloth' (1818).

56 Alice Barnaby, *Light Touches: Cultural Practices of Illumination, 1800–1900* (London, 2017), p. 51.

57 Ibid., p. 65.

58 Andreas Blühm and Louise Lippincott, *Light! The Industrial Age, 1750–1900: Art and Science, Technology and Society* (London, 2000), pp. 232–3.

59 Thomas Makepeace Thackeray, *The History of Pendennis* (London, 1848), chap. 51.

60 Ian McKeever, 'Whistler's Whites: Creating Presence with a Pared Down Palette', www.royalacademy.org.uk, 6 May 2022.

FIVE Underwear and Dirt

1 Judith Flanders, *Inside the Victorian Home* (London, 2003), p. 309.

2 Ibid., p. 306.

3 Karen Bowman, *Corsets and Codpieces: A Social History of Outrageous Fashion* (London, 2015).

4 R. Rushworth, *The Bum Shop*, 1785, hand-coloured etching.

5 Cited in Kat Eschner, 'Although Less Deadly than Crinolines, Bustles Were Still a Pain in the Behind', *Smithsonian Magazine* (21 April 2017).

6 Mimi Matthews, 'The Trouble with Bustles', https://firstnighthistory.wordpress.com, 5 March 2016.

7 Barbara Pym, *Some Tame Gazelle* (London, 1950), chap. 1.

8 Victoria Patterson, 'Socks and Underthings: Desire, Seduction, and the Private Life of Spinsters in Some Tame Gazelle', paper presented at the 18th North American Conference of the Barbara Pym Society, Cambridge, MA, 12–13 March 2016, https://barbara-pym.org, accessed 24 June 2020.

9 Elizabeth Wilson, *Adorned in Dreams: Fashion and Modernity* (London, 2003), p. 106.

10 From the web page of Urbody, https://urbody.co, a company specializing in non-binary underwear.

11 Priya Elan, 'The Non-Binary Underwear Company that Wants to "Degender" Fashion', *The Guardian*, www.theguardian.com, 8 May 2021.

12 Cecil and Phillis Cunnington, *The History of Underclothes* (London, 1951), chap. 3.

13 Dan Piepenbring, 'A Brief History of the Codpiece, the Personal Protection for Renaissance Equipment', *New Yorker*, 23 May 2020.

14 Sicillo Araldo, 'Trattato del colori nelle arme, nelle livre et nelle divise' [1565], cited ibid.

15 C. M. Misson, *Memoirs and Observations in His Travels Over England* [in French, 1698], trans. Mr Ozell (London, 1719), p. 303.

16 Beverly Gordon, *Textiles: The Whole Story – Uses, Meanings, Significance* (London, 2011), p. 25.

17 Carole Rawcliffe, *Leprosy in Medieval England* (Woodbridge, 2006), p. 280.

18 Michele Nicole Robinson, 'Dirty Laundry: Caring for Clothing in Early Modern Italy', *Costume*, LV/1 (2021), www.euppublishing.com, accessed 5 April 2021.

19 Agnes Allen, *The Story of Clothes* (London, 1967), p. 212.

20 David Cecil, *Max: A Biography* (London, 1964), p. 425, cited in Penelope Byrde, *The Male Image: Men's Fashion in Britain, 1300–1970* (London, 1999), p. 98.

21 Stella Gibbons, *Cold Comfort Farm* (London, 1932), chap. 1.

22 Sheila Heti et al., eds, *Women in Clothes* (London, 2014): Benedicte Pinset, p. 240; Aria Sloss, p. 466; Leanne Shapton, p. 496.

23 Catriona McPherson, *Dandy Gilver and a Bothersome Number of Corpses* (London, 2012), chap. 7, quoted in 'Dress Down Sunday:

Underwear On the Line', www.clothesinbooks.blogspot.com,
9 September 2012.

24 Ernest Mason Satow, *A Diplomat in Japan: The Diaries of Ernest
Satow* [1921] (London, 2002), p. 74.

25 Alison Matthews David, 'Tainted Love: Oscar Wilde's Toxic Green
Carnation, Queerness, and Chromophobia', in *Colors in Fashion*, ed.
Jonathan Faiers and Mary Westerman Bulgarella (London, 2016), p. 131.

26 Nina Edwards, *Dressed for War: Uniform, Civilian Clothing and
Trappings, 1914–1918* (London, 2015), pp. 93–4.

27 Ibid., p. 79.

28 Lyn MacDonald, *They Called it Passchendaele: The Story of the Third
Battle of Ypres and of the Men Who Fought In It* [1978] (London, 1993),
p. 80, quoting the testimony of W. Worrell, Rifleman.

29 Kate Adie, *Corsets to Camouflage: Women and War* (London, 2003),
p. 68.

30 Gene Demby, 'Sagging Pants and the Long History of "Dangerous"
Street Fashion', www.npr.org, 11 September 2014.

31 Aritha van Herk, 'Invisibled Laundry', *Signs*, XXVII/3 (Spring 2002),
pp. 893–900.

32 Ibid., p. 897.

33 Quentin Crisp, *The Naked Civil Servant* (London, 1968).

SIX Meringues and Sleek Satin Shifts

1 A suggestion made by Alison Lurie, *The Language of Clothes*
(London, 1981), p. 186.

2 Teresa Anne Hiener, 'Shinto Wedding, Samurai Bride: Inventing
Tradition and Fashioning Identity in the Rituals of Bridal Dress
in Japan', PhD thesis, Pittsburgh University, 1997.

3 Queen Victoria, Journal Entry, 10 February 1840,
www.queenvictoriasjournals.org.

4 C. Willett Cunnington, *English Women's Clothing in the Present
Century* (London, 1952), p. 43.

5 Nina Tarasova of the Costume Department at the State Hermitage
Museum, St Petersburg, email to author, 5 October 2021.

6 Nina Edwards, *On the Button: The Significance of an Ordinary Item*
(London, 2012), pp. xxiv–xxvii.

7 Frommer quoted in 'A Wedding Dress from Parachute Silk', *Wisconsin
State Journal*, 5 August 1943, p. 12.

8 'Wedding Gown Made from a White Rayon Parachute Worn by
Multiple Jewish Brides in a DP Camp', https://collections.ushmm.org,
accessed 5 December 2021.

SEVEN High Fashion and Street Fashion

1 Dodie Smith, *It Ends with Revelations* (London, 1967), in the chapter 'Night of the Long Gloves'.

2 Thorstein Veblen, *The Theory of the Leisure Class* [1899] (New York, 1994), p. 110.

3 'Elegant to the last and always dressed in white', in 'Italian Ballet Star Carla Fracci Dies Age 84', www.france24.com, 27 May 2021.

4 Anke Bernau, *Girls on Film: Medieval Virginity in the Cinema* (Jefferson, MO, 2004), p. 100.

5 The equivalent of about £25,000 in 2023.

6 'Story of a Dress: "Top Hat"', www.screenchic.com, 1 September 2020.

7 Nina Edwards, *Dressed for War: Uniform, Civilian Clothing and Trappings, 1914–1918* (London, 2015), pp. 49–50.

8 Denis Diderot, *Encyclopédie*, vol. IV, p. 428, and vol. X, p. 474, cited in June Swan et al., *Birds of Paradise: Plumes and Feathers in Fashion*, exh. cat., MoMu, Antwerp (2014), p. 190.

9 Chanel quoted ibid., p. 123.

10 Christian Dior, *Dior by Dior*, trans. Antonia Fraser (London, 1957), p. 40.

11 Judith Watt, *Vogue On: Elsa Schiaparelli* (London, 2012), p. 146.

12 Julie Tong, '34 Vogue Editors Share the Best White T-Shirts', www.vogue.com, 8 July 2022.

13 April Masini, *Date Out of Your League* (Beverly Hills, CA, 2003), p. 60.

14 Caroline Davies, 'Ex-BBC Reporter Martin Bell Praises Surgeons Who Rebuilt His Face', www.theguardian.com, 9 January 2019.

15 Chanel quote in Amy de la Haye, *Chanel* (London, 2011).

16 Madeleine Delpierre, *Dress in France in the Eighteenth Century* (London, 1998), p. 1.

17 De la Haye, *Chanel*, p. 51.

18 Kimberly Wahl, 'Purity and Parity: The White Dress of the Suffrage Movement in Early Twentieth Century Britain', in *Colors in Fashion*, ed. Jonathan Faiers and Mary Westerman Bulgarella (London, 2017), p. 21.

19 'The Suffragette and the Dress Problem', *Votes for Women*, 21 (30 July 1908), p. 348.

20 Ibid., p. 32, citing Emmeline Pethick-Lawrence, one of the driving forces behind the promotional use of colour, *My Part in a Changing World* (London, 1938).

21 'How Wearing White Became a Symbol of Female Solidarity', *AnOther*, www.anothermag.com, 4 January 2019.

22 Hamish Bowles, *Jacqueline Kennedy: The White House Years* (New York, 2001), p. 75.

23 F. Scott Fitzgerald, *The Great Gatsby* (New York, 1925), chap. 1.

24 Dior, *Dior by Dior*, p. 14.

25 Ibid., p. 76.

26 Ibid., p. 94.

27 Ibid., p. 109.

28 Susan Stewart, *On Longing: Narratives of the Miniature, the Gigantic, the Souvenir, the Collection* [1993] (Baltimore, MD, 2005), p. 57.

29 Nimreth Sidhu et al., 'What Colour Should I Wear? How Clothing Colour Affects Women's Judgements of Other Women's Body Attractiveness and Body Size', *Acta Psychologica*, CCXVIII (July 2021), pp. 1–8.

EIGHT Whiteout

1 Benjamin Black, *Christine Falls* (London, 2006), p. 10.

2 William Huttmann, *The Life of Jesus Christ Including His Apocryphal History* (London, 1818), p. 90. The Syndonia story appears in de Worde's 1509 version of the Gospel of Nicodemus, *Early English Books online*, pp. 22–4.

3 'Ancient Egypt: Egyptian Mummies', Smithsonian Museum of Natural History, www.si.edu, accessed 18 July 2021.

4 Dominic Montserrat, *Akhenaten: History, Fantasy and Ancient Egypt* (London, 2000).

5 Phillis Cunnington, *Costume for Births, Marriages and Deaths* (London, 1972), pp. 41–3, 55.

6 'François Clouet, *Mary, Queen of Scots*', www.rct.uk, accessed 6 July 2022.

7 Mary G. Houston, *Medieval Costume in England and France: The 13th, 14th and 15th Centuries* [1939] (London, 1996), p. 117.

8 Lou Taylor, *Mourning Dress: A Costume and Social History* (London, 2009), p. 85.

9 Angela Thirkell, *The Brandons* (London, 1939).

10 Nina Tarasova of the Costume Department at The State Hermitage Museum, St Petersburg, email to author, 5 October 2021.

11 'Death: The Last Taboo', https://australian.museum, accessed 4 March 2021.

12 Beverly Gordon, *Textiles: The Whole Story – Uses, Meanings, Significance* (London, 2011), p. 257.

13 Valery Garrett, *Chinese Dress from the Qing Dynasty to the Present* (Rutland, VT, 2007), p. 124.

14 Zack Davisson, *Yurei: The Japanese Ghost* (Seattle, WA, 2014), p. 83.

15 Reminiscent of the distinction in Western dress where men wear their jackets left side over right and women vice versa. It can feel wrong for either sex to be buttoned up the other way. Significantly, it seems less out of place for a woman to be dressed left over right and might even gain her a certain cross-gender allure, whereas the opposite is sometimes found more perturbing for a man.

16 Mike Dash, 'Ghosts, Witches, Vampires, Fairies and the Law of Murder', Charles Fort Institute, 25 June 2010, https://mikedas hhistory.com.

17 The film was adapted from a story in Pu Songling's *Strange Tales of a Chinese Studio*, his collection from 1740 of supernatural tales set in ancient China.

18 Jack Hartnell, *Medieval Bodies: Life, Death and Art in the Middle Ages* (London, 2018), p. 103.

19 Alan Stewart, *The Oxford History of Life Writing* (Oxford, 2018), vol. II, p. 228.

20 Christopher Hibbert, *Queen Victoria: A Personal History* (London, 1978), p. 497.

21 Georgina Howell, *Diana: Her Life in Fashion* (London, 1998), p. 105

22 Mark Twain, *Maxims by Mark Twain*, ed. Merle Johnson (New York, 1927).

Bibliography

Adam, H., and A. D. Galinsky, 'Enclothed Cognition', *Journal of Experimental Social Psychology*, LXVII/4 (July 2012), www.sciencedirect.com

Amelekhina, Svetlana A., and Alexey K. Levykin, *Magnificence of the Tsars: Ceremonial Men's Dress of the Russian Imperial Court, 1721–1917* (London, 2008)

Ashelford, Jane, *The Art of Dress* (London, 1996)

Baecque, Antoine de, and Noel Herpe, *Eric Rohmer: A Biography*, trans. Steven Randall and Lisa Neal (New York, 2016)

Bari, Shahidha, *Dressed: The Philosophy of Clothes* (London, 2020)

Barnaby, Alice, *Light Touches: Cultural Practices of Illumination, 1800–1900* (London, 2017)

Baxter, Denise Amy, ed., *In the Age of Empire: A Cultural History of Dress and Fashion* (London, 2017)

Bell, Quentin, *On Human Finery* (London, 1976)

Birbari, Elizabeth, *Dress in Italian Painting, 1460–1500* (London, 1975)

Bland, Alexander, *The Nureyev Image* (London, 1976)

Blühm, Andreas, and Louise Lippincott, *Light! The Industrial Age, 1750–1900: Art and Science, Technology and Society* (London, 2000)

Bond, Sarah, 'The Revealing History of the Fig Leaf', *Forbes*, www.forbes.com, 27 October 2021

Bowles, Hamish, *Jacqueline Kennedy: The White House Years* (New York, 2001)

Bruna, Denis, ed., *Fashioning the Body: An Intimate History of the Silhouette* (New York, 2015)

Bucar, Elizabeth, *Pious Fashion: How Muslim Women Dress* (London, 2017)

Buruma, Anna, *Fashions of the Past: A Historical Guide to World
Costumes* (London, 1999)

Byrde, Penelope, *The Male Image: Men's Fashion in Britain, 1300–1970*
(London, 1979)

Chakrabarty, Dipesh, 'Clothing the Political Man: A Reading of the
Use of Khadi/White in Indian Public Life', *Postcolonial Studies*,
IV/1 (2001), pp. 27–38

Chrisman-Campbell, Kimberly, *Fashion Victims: Dress
at the Court of Louis XVI and Marie Antoinette, 1774–1793*
(London, 2015)

Cleland, Liza, Mary Harlow and Lloyd Llewellyn-Jones, eds,
The Clothed Body in the Ancient World (Oxford, 2005)

Collins, Wilkie, *The Woman in White* (London, 1859)

Croom, Alexandra, *Roman Clothing and Fashion* (Stroud, 2010)

Cunnington, C. Willett, *Why Women Wear Clothes* (London, 1941)

De la Haye, Amy, and Elizabeth Wilson, *Defining Dress: Dress as Object,
Meaning and Identity* (New York, 1999)

Dior, Christian, *Dior by Dior*, trans. Antonia Fraser (London, 1957)

Edwards, Nina, *Dressed for War: Uniform, Civilian Clothing and
Trappings, 1914 to 1918* (London, 2015)

——, *On the Button: The Significance of an Ordinary Item*
(London, 2012)

Ehrman, Edwina, *The Wedding Dress: 300 Years of Bridal Fashions*
(London, 2011)

Erler, Mary C., 'Margery Kempe's White Clothes', *Medium Aevum*,
LXII (Oxford, 1993)

Evans, Maria Millington, *Chapters on Greek Dress* (London, 1893)

Faber Oestreich, Kate, 'Fashioning Chastity: British Marriage Plots
and the Tailoring of Desire, 1789–1928', PhD thesis, Ohio State
University, Columbus, Ohio (2008)

Faiers, Jonathan, and Mary Westerman Bulgarella, eds, *Colors in Fashion*
(London, 2017)

Fairweather, Janet, *Liber Eliensis: A History of the Isle of Ely from the
Seventh Century to the Twelfth Century, Compiled by a Monk of Ely
in the Twelfth Century* (Woodbridge, 1995)

Fanfani, Giovanni, Mary Harlow and Marie-Louise Nosch, eds, *Spinning
Fates and the Song of the Loom: The Use of Textiles, Clothing and Cloth
Production as Metaphor, Symbol and Narrative Device in Greek and
Latin Literature* (Oxford, 2016)

Fields, Jill, *An Intimate Affair: Women, Lingerie, and Sexuality*
(Berkeley, CA, 2007)

Fischer, Marina, 'Ancient Greek Prostitutes and the Textile Industry
in Attic Vase-Painting *c.* 550–450 BCE', *Classical World*, CVI/2
(Winter 2013), pp. 219–59

Gallo, Marzia Cataldi, *Il Papa e le sue vesti: da Paolo V a Giovanni Paolo II,
1600–2000* (Vatican City, 2016)

Garrett, Valery, *Chinese Dress: From the Qing Dynasty to the Present*
(Rutland, VT, 2007)

Garrison, Daniel H., ed., *A Cultural History of the Human Body in
Antiquity* (Oxford, 2010)

Geczy, Adam, and Vicki Karaminas, eds, *Fashion and Art* (Oxford, 2012)

Gent, Lucy, and Nigel Llewellyn, eds, *Renaissance Bodies: The Human
Figure in English Culture, c. 1540–1660* (London, 1990)

Gordon, Beverly, *Textiles: The Whole Story – Uses, Meanings, Significance*
(London, 2011)

Harlow, Mary, ed., *A Cultural History of Dress and Fashion: In Antiquity*
(London, 2017)

Hartnell, Jack, *Medieval Bodies: Life, Death and Art in the Middle Ages*
(London, 2018)

Harvey, John, *Men in Black* (London, 1995)

Heller, Sarah-Grace, ed., *A Cultural History of Dress and Fashion*
(London, 2017)

Hibbert, Christopher, *Queen Victoria, A Personal History* (London, 2008)

Hill, Colleen, *Fairy Tale Fashion* (London, 2016)

Hope, Thomas, *Costumes of the Greeks and Romans* [1812] (New York,
2000)

Houston, Mary G., *Medieval Costume in England and France: The 13th,
14th and 15th Centuries* [1939] (London, 1996)

Ireland, William Henry, *The Life of Napoleon Bonaparte*, vol. IV
(London, 1828)

Jarus, Owen, 'Rare Ancient Statue Depicts Topless Female Gladiator',
www.livescience.com, 17 April 2012

Jenkins, David, ed., *The Cambridge History of Western Textiles*
(Cambridge, 2003)

Jones, Colin, *The Great Nation: France from Louis XV to Napoleon*
(London, 2003)

Kuhns, Elizabeth, *The Habit: A History of the Clothing of Catholic Nuns*
(London, 2003)

Kundera, Milan, *The Unbearable Lightness of Being* (London, 1984)

Laver, James, *Costume* (London, 1963)

Lee, John S., *The Medieval Clothier* (Belfast, 2018)

Lurie, Alison, *The Language of Clothes* (London, 1981)

McFadden, David Revere, *Radical Lace and Subversive Knitting*
  (New York, 2010)
Mackenzie, Mairi, *Dream Suits: The Wonderful World of Nudie Cohn*
  (Antwerp, 2012)
McNeil, Peter, *A Cultural History of Dress and Fashion: In the Age of the
  Enlightenment* (London, 2017)
——, *The Twentieth Century to Today: Fashion: Critical and Primary
  Sources*, vol. IV (Oxford, 2009)
——, ed., *The Nineteenth Century, Fashion: Critical and Primary Sources*,
  vol. III (Oxford, 2009)
Maddocks, Fiona, *Hildegard of Bingen: The Woman of Her Age*
  (London, 2001)
Magilton, John, et al., eds, *Lepers Outside the Gate: Excavations at
  the Cemetery of the Hospital of St James and St Mary Magdalene,
  Chichester 1986–7 and 1993* (York, 2008)
Mann, Jill, *Chaucer and Medieval Estates Satire: The Literature
  of Social Classes and the General Prologue to the Canterbury Tales*
  (Cambridge, 1973)
Miller-Spillman, Kimberly A., Andrew Reilly and Patricia Hunt-Hurst,
  eds, *The Meaning of Dress*, 3rd edn (London, 2012)
Mills, Harrianne, 'Greek Clothing Regulations: Sacred and Profane?,
  Zeitschrift fur Papyrologie und Epigraphik (January 1984),
  pp. 255–65
Moore, Alfred S., *Linen: From the Raw Material to the Finished Product*
  (London, 1954)
Moore, Doris Langley, *Gallery of Fashion, 1790–1822* (London, 1949)
Olson, Kelly, *Masculinity and Dress in Roman Antiquity* (London, 2017)
Parker, Rozsika, *The Subversive Stitch: Embroidery and the Making
  of the Feminine* [1984] (London, 1996)
Rauser, Amelia, *The Age of Undress: Art, Fashion and the Classical Ideal
  in the 1790s* (London, 2020)
Rawcliffe, Carole, *Leprosy in Medieval England* (Woodbridge, 2006)
Rösener, Werner, *Peasants in the Middle Ages*, trans. Alexander Stutzer
  (London, 1992)
Salazar, Ligaya, *Fashion v Sport* (London, 2008)
Schoeser, Mary, and Celia Rufey, *English and American Textiles from
  1790 to the Present* (London, 1989)
Scott, Margaret, *Medieval Dress and Fashion* (London, 2007)
Steele, Valerie, *The Corset: A Cultural History* (London, 2003)
Stewart, Susan, *On Longing: Narratives of the Miniature, the Gigantic,
  the Souvenir, the Collection* [1993] (Baltimore, MD, 2005)

Strutt, J., *The Dress and Habits of the People of England* (London, 1842),
vols I and II

Swan, June, et al., *Birds of Paradise: Plumes and Feathers in Fashion*,
exh. cat., MoMu, Antwerp (2014)

Talbot, Alice-Mary, and Denis F. Sullivan, trans. and eds, *The History
of Leo the Deacon: Byzantine Military Expansion in the Tenth Century*
(Washington, DC, 2005)

Tymorek, Stan, ed., *Clotheslines: A Collection of Poetry and Art*
(New York, 2001)

Van Buren, Anne H., *Illuminating Fashion: Dress in the Art of Medieval
France and the Netherlands, 1325–1515* (New York, 2011)

Van Herk, Aritha, 'Invisibled Laundry', *Signs*, XXVII/3 (Spring 2002),
pp. 893–900

Veblen, Thorstein, *The Theory of the Leisure Class* [1899] (New York, 1994)

Watt, Judith, *Ossie Clark, 1965–74* (London, 2003)

Whitelock, Anna, *Elizabeth's Bedfellows: An Intimate History of the
Queen's Court* (London, 2013)

Williams, Abigail, 'A Brief History of Modesty', *La Mesure et l'excès, Revue
de la Société d'études anglo-américaines des XVII et XVIII*, 71 (2014),
pp. 135–56, www.journals.openedition.org, accessed July 2021

Williams, Gordon Willis, 'Roman Marriage Ceremonies', in *Oxford
Classical Dictionary* (Oxford, 2015)

Wilson, Elizabeth, *Love Game: A History of Tennis, from Victorian Pastime
to Global Phenomenon* (London, 2014)

Wilson, Matthew R. 'Speechless Spectacles: Commedia Pantomime
in France, England, and the Americas During the Eighteenth and
Nineteenth Centuries', in *The Routledge Companion to Commedia
dell'Arte*, ed. Judith Chaffee and Olly Crick (London, 2017)

Acknowledgements

With many thanks for the information, material and opportunity to discuss this book: Philip Attwood; Bea Bradley; Judith Bronkhurst; Nellie Collier; Annet Couwenberg; Deanna Dahisad, antiques dealer; Brigitte Dold; Jenny Domone; Peter Edwards; Lisa Fisher; Josie Floyd; Pip Frost; Pamela Gould; Gregory Grey; Caroline Jansen; Oliver Leaman; the London Library; Carol Miles; Jane and Graham Reddish; Judy Roberts; Nina Tarasova of the Costume Department, the State Hermitage Museum, St Petersburg; Dick Vigers; Michela Vignali; Zikun Zhang. Grateful thanks also to Michael Leaman and all at Reaktion Books, including Alex Ciobanu and Martha Jay.

Photo Acknowledgements

The author and publishers wish to express their thanks to the below sources of illustrative material and/or permission to reproduce it. Some locations of artworks are also given below, in the interest of brevity:

Art Institute of Chicago: pp. 115, 123, 170, 181; Brooklyn Museum, New York: p. 32; The Clark Art Institute, Williamstown, MA: p. 166 (top); collection of the author: pp. 8 (bottom), 44; © Annet Couwenberg, photo Dan Meyers: p. 167 (bottom); courtesy Deanna Dahlsad, kitsch-slapped.com: p. 129; Dallas Museum of Art, TX: p. 33; Davison Art Center, Wesleyan University, Middletown, CT: pp. 30 (photo M. Johnston), 37 (photo R. Lee); Heritage Auctions, Ha.com: p. 167 (top); The J. Paul Getty Museum, Los Angeles: pp. 13, 24, 59; Library of Congress, Prints and Photographs Division, Washington, DC: pp. 9, 11, 31, 35, 60, 120, 140; The Metropolitan Museum of Art, New York: pp. 21, 22, 128; Musée Carnavalet – Histoire de Paris: p. 136; Musée du Pays de Hanau, Bouxwiller: p. 12; Museum Rotterdam: p. 156 (CC BY-SA 3.0 NL); National Gallery of Art, Washington, DC: pp. 103, 116, 164; National Museum, Kraków: p. 165; The New York Public Library: p. 69; Petit Palais – Musée des Beaux-Arts de la Ville de Paris: p. 108; courtesy Jane Reddish: pp. 45, 99, 122; © Paula Rego, courtesy the artist and Victoria Miro, London and Venice: pp. 148, 168; Rijksmuseum, Amsterdam: pp. 76, 90, 101, 117, 124, 183; Robert S. Cox Special Collections and University Archives Research Center, University of Massachusetts Amherst Libraries: p. 6; Royal Collection Trust/© His Majesty King Charles III 2023: pp. 121, 188; The Walters Art Museum, Baltimore, MD: p. 16; Wellcome Collection, London: pp. 8 (top), 38, 41, 80, 82, 84, 118, 155; Wikimedia Commons: pp. 19 (photo Miguel Hermoso Cuesta, CC BY-SA 3.0), 158 (photo Allan Warren, CC BY 3.0); Yale Center for British Art, New Haven, CT: pp. 74, 93, 114, 161, 162; Yale University Art Gallery, New Haven, CT: pp. 100, 163, 166 (bottom), 191.

Index

Page numbers in *italics* refer to illustrations

Adam and Eve 19
Agniel, Marguerite *155*
Alinejad, Masih, 'My Stealthy
    Freedom' campaign 39–40
ancient clothing 17–18, 25, 28,
    101, 107
    Egyptian 18, 20–23, *22*
    Greek 18, 23
    Minoan 23
    Roman 17, 23, *24*, 25,
        26–7; brothels 26;
        Olympic Games 27
Austen, Jane 104
    Mansfield Park 105–6
    Northanger Abbey 104–5
    Pride and Prejudice 106

baptism 29, 31, *31*, 154
Basic Instinct 181
Bathsheba 53–4
Baudelaire, Charles 109–10
Bell, Martin 176
Belle de Jour 145
Bertin, Rose 70, 89, 184
Boswell, James 137

Brando, Marlon *174*
Brontë, Charlotte, *Jane Eyre* 112–14
Brummell, George (Beau) 115–16
Brynner, Yul *96*
bustle 127–8, *128*, 131
The Bum Shop 128

Chakrabarty, Dipesh 14
Chanel, Coco 6–8, 10, 172–4,
    177, 182
Charlemagne 61–2, 84
Chinnery, George, *An English
    Family in Macao* 114
Christina of Markyate 62
Chronicles of Narnia, The 171
class, indicator of 23, 25–6, 62, 135,
    138
    Korea, white for commoners 56
    Robert Dudley, Earl of
    Leicester 71
    spinning and weaving 26
    white glove buildings 76
Clouet, François, *Mary, Queen
    of Scots* 188
codpiece 70, 131–2, 134–5

Cohn, Nudie 176
Cold Comfort Farm 138
Collins, Wilkie, *The Woman in White* 110–11
Confirmation 9
Constable, John, *Mary Freer 161*
corsetry 101
    brassière 131, 133, 134, 139, 142
    Bridget Jones's Diary 132
    modern 130
    and Paul Poiret 130
    roll-on 128
cotton 90, 100, 101, 107, 126
    fichu 98, 106
    Gone with the Wind 122
    muslin *38*, 92, 102, 107–8, 118
Couwenberg, Annet, *Dutch Ruffled Collar 167*
cravat 80, 81, 92, 94, 98, 104, 116–17
    Brian Dillon 117
    H. Le Blanc's treatise 138
    Napoleon 97
cricket 7, 43–4, *44*, 47, 159–60, 178
crinoline 121–3, 126–7, 150
    panier 125–6
croquet 45, 47
Cruikshank, Isaac 107

dandy 115, *115*, 137–8
dark clothing 10, 12–14, 27, 39, 40, 65
Daumier, Honoré, *The Phantom 30*
David, Alison Matthews 142
David, Jacques-Louis, *The Emperor Napoleon in His Study at the Tuileries 116*
Davies, Glenys 23
De Carlo, Yvonne, as Lily Munster *88*
Degas, Edgar, *Yellow Dancers (In the Wings) 170*
Delacroix, Eugène, *Marguerite's Ghost Appearing to Faust 191*

Delpierre, Madeleine 89, 178
Deneuve, Catherine *145*
dentistry 49–50
Devis, Arthur, *Mr and Mrs Hill 93*
Dickens, Charles
    exploding bustle 128
    Great Expectations 111–12
Dior, Christian 95–6, 174, 182–3
doctors' dress 48–51, *82, 83*
Doyle, William M. S., *Young Lady in a Sheer White Dress 100*

Ehrman, Edwina 149–50
elastic 127, 129, 130, 131, 132, 137
Electric Horseman, The 175–6
Elizabeth I, Queen 65
embroidery 98, 102
    Mary Wollstonecraft 98
    whitework 98, 109, 119, 126
Erickson, Carolly 75
Evans, Maria Millington 23

feathers 55, 71, 75, 85, 86, 87, 109
    plumassiers 171–2
    Top Hat 171–2
First Communion *8*, 9, 61
Fischer, Marina 26
Flanders, Judith 126
footwear
    boots *157*, 160
    co-respondents 178
    crackows 54–5
    duck-bills 56
    patent 178
    sportswear 178
    trainers 119, 138, 145, 175, 178
Fracci, Carla 170–71
Frozen 171
fuller 23, 27, 32, 39
fur 38, 75, 95–6, 150, 195

Gainsborough, Thomas
    Mr and Mrs Andrews 102, 104
    Mr and Mrs William Hallett 103
Gandhi, Mahatma, khadi clothing
    14
Gérard, Baron François-Pascal-
    Simon, *Alexandrine Émilie
    Brongniart 163*
Gheeraerts the Younger, Marcus 65
Gibson Girl 123
gloves 39, 50, 75–8, 80–81
Great Gatsby, The 181
Great Male Renunciation of Colour
    13
grubbiness 9, 137, *174*, *175*
    and germs 141

Hannibal's Spanish infantry 40
Hardy, Thomas, *Tess of the
    d'Urbervilles* 107
Hartnell, Norman 194
hats 95–7, 150
    Alpini 172
    fur 96
    papakha 96
Miss Havisham 111
Hazlitt, William 93–4, 109
Highmore, Joseph, *Mrs Sharpe and
    Her Child 162*
Hildegard of Bingen 36
hosiery 39, 60, 65–6, 78, 132, 138,
    178–9
    footless 66
    Gustave Flaubert 80–81
    Henry VIII 55
    Napoleon 94, 97, *116*
    William Lee 66
Howell, Georgina 194

Igorevich, Sviatoslav, Grand Prince
    of Kiev 42

innocence 7, 30–31, 54, 73, 78, 135,
    153, 170
    babies' 135
    and economic crash of 1929 10
    old age 144–5
    wedding dresses 121, 148
Ivanhoe 54

James Bond 14
Japanese white lace punk 88
Joan of Arc 171

Keller, Clare Waight 152
Kempe, Margery 61
Kennedy, Jacqueline 180
Khan, Imran and Reham 15
Kirchner, Ernst Ludwig, *Girl
    in White Chemise* 166
Knights Templar 39, 57
Korean *chima jeogori* 55–6
Ku Klux Klan 9–10, *9*

lace 10, 29, 46, 108, *108*, 194
    and Napoleon 109
laundry 7, 24–5, 27, 60–61, 66–7,
    72, 135–7, 146
    Aritha van Herk, secrets of 146
    bleaching 12, 22, 25, 27, 32, 58,
    63, 141, 160
    Egypt, men's work 59
    First World War 142
    frequency 60–61
    goffering 68
    ironing 59–60
    pressing 24–5
    rinsing 25, 58, 135, *136*
    soap 39, 60, 135
    and status 139–41
Lawrence of Arabia 171
leper 63–4, 136
Lily Munster 88, *88*

linen 126, 135, *136*, 138, 192
    attifet 187
    barbe 187
    Egyptian mummies 186
    fichu 98–9, *103*, *106*
    ruff 39, 66–7, 72, *76*, *101*, 102
    wimple 48, 187
Little Women 78
loincloth 19, 20, 21, 43, 64, 68
Lythgoe, Nigel *158*

macaroni 94, 116
McQueen, Alexander 152
Maes, Nicholas, *The Lace-Maker*
    108
Malczewski, Jacek, self-portrait
    165
A Man Trap 38
Man in the White Suit, The 119, *167*
Marchal, Charles-François, *The*
    Servants' Fair at Bouxwiller 12
Marie Antoinette 85, 86, 89, 90–92,
    90, 102
Mary, Queen of Scots 150, 187, *188*
Medici, Catherine de 187
military uniform 13, 23, 39, 40
Monroe, Marilyn *173*
Monserrat, Dominic 187
Moore, Albert Joseph, *Lilies 166*
Morisot, Berthe, *Woman at Her*
    Toilette 181
mourning 150, 187
    deuil blanc 187
    Queen Victoria 194
Mytens, Jacob de Witte, *Lord*
    of Haamstede 117

Napoleon 94, 97, 109, 116–17,
    116
nightclothes 39, 138, 144, 153
Nureyev, Rudolf 169

nursing 7, 14, 31, 49, 50–51
    The Flying Nun 48–9
    Nightingale, Florence 48

Olson, Kelly 25, 27

Pandora fashion doll 183–4, *183*
Paris ateliers 160
Parker, Rozsika 98
pearl 15, 33, 42, 55, 57, 65–6, 151,
    178, 180, 187
    Armada portrait 75
Performance 171
petticoat 99, 142
    farthingale 125
    panier 124, 125–6
Phantom Thread 169
Pickenoy, Nicolaes Eliasz, *Johanna*
    le Maire 76
Pils, Isidore Alexandre Augustin,
    Place Pigalle, Paris 136
polo 47–8
pornography 146
purity 36, 58, 107
    nightwear 144–5
Pym, Barbara, *Some Tame Gazelle*
    130

Queen Charlotte's Ball 77–8

rap artist 176
Rego, Paula
    Bride 148
    Girdle 168
religious significance 32–40
    Christianity 31–2, 37, 64
    Druidism 3
    Islam 39
    Jainism 33
    Judaism 34
    Latter Day Saints 39

monks 37–9
nuns *8*, 34–6, *35*, 39, 48–9
Zoroastrianism 33
Ribeiro, Aileen, 101, 108–9
rikishi wrestler 43
Rohmer, Éric, *A Winter's Tale* 73
Royal Engineers, Singapore *41*

Sargent, John Singer, *Mrs George
    Swinton (Elizabeth Ebsworth)*
    123
Satow, Ernest 141
Schiaparelli, Elsa 95–6, 175
Scott, Margaret 53
Selfe, Daphne 87
servants 12–13, 80, 99
Seven Year Itch, The 171, *173*
sewing 98–9, 119–21, 160, 169, 184
    machines 121
Shakespeare, William
    As You Like It 75
    Hamlet 73
    Love's Labour's Lost 75
    Much Ado About Nothing 177
    The Taming of the Shrew 73
    The Winter's Tale 73–4
shirt 58, 78, 129, 137–8
    business 13
    IBM corporate 10
    Oreos 34
    white-collar workers 42
shroud 10, 19, 113–14, 121, 185, 192
    of Turin 185–6
silk 65, 71, 80, 85, 101, 102, 104, 106
    effect of French Revolution 107,
    108
silver *155*, *162*, 171, 181
Spark, Muriel, *The Abbess of Crewe*
    36
stockings 66, 80, 94, 97
A Streetcar Named Desire 174

suffragettes 179
suit, white 28, 40
    Alexandria Ocasio-Cortez 180
    Geraldine Ferraro 180
    grooms 157
    Hillary Clinton 180
    Marlene Dietrich 28
    Miami Vice 28
    Officer and a Gentleman, An 42
    safari suit 14
    Saturday Night Fever 28, 43
sumptuary laws 54–5, 61–3, 134
swaddling 21, 31, *37*, 38, 135, 193

tailoring 102–3, 108, 178
Taras Bulba 96
Tarasova, Nina 153–4
tennis 44–7, *45*
    Gertrude Moran 46
    Suzanne Lenglen 44–5
    Teddy Tinling 45–6
Tiggy-Winkle, Mrs 58
Tissot, James, *Woe unto You, Scribes
    and Pharisees* 32
T-shirt 13, 119, 129, 140, 175
Turkish *nefis* 40
Twain, Mark 195

understated male fashion 94–5
underwear 57, 65–6, 101–2, 107,
    133–4, 141–2, *145*, 146
    braies 133
    erotic 137, *145*, 145–6
    First World War 142–3
    fundoshi 141, 145
    mamillare bands 57
    non-binary 133
    outerwear 140
    Paula Rego *148*, *168*
    as protection 144
    Saggers 143–4

shapewear 132
VPL 130

Veblen, Thorstein 79, 114, 139–40, 160
veil *103*, 111, 113, 150–51
    bridal 147, *148*, 148–9
    Elizabeth I 65, 67
    film costume 54, 189
    First Communion 9
    Homer 23, 26
    and modesty 134
    Queen Victoria 194
    virginity 36
    widows 188
à la victime fashion 92
Victoria, Queen 121, *121*, 150–51, 153, 194
Vigée Le Brun, Elisabeth, portrait 89–92, 100
Vreeland, Diana 10

War, funk band 10
wedding garb *124*, 147–57
    Catherine Middleton 152, 153
    China 149
    Diana Spencer 151–2
    Elizabeth Bowes-Lyon 151, 194
    First World War 154
    Imperial Russia 153–4
    Meghan Markle 152
    Miss Havisham 111
    parachute fabric 154–6, *156*
    Queen Victoria *121*, 150–51, 153

West Side Story 180
Weyden, Rogier van der, *Portrait of a Lady 103*
Whistler, James McNeill 123
    Symphony in White, No. 1: The White Girl 164
white-coat syndrome 50
White Sheik, The 171
wigs 79–88, *80*, *84*
    and Emma Bovary 80–81
    Humphrey Ravenscroft, perms 83
    legal 82
    Louis XIV, King of France 83
    Schitt's Creek 88
Wilde, Oscar, *The Importance of Being Earnest* 87
Wodehouse, P. G. 51–2
wool 7, 20, 23, 26–8, 37, 56, *60*, 66, 71
    Athena 26
    Chaucer 63
    harbouring lice 133
    Muslim pilgrims 39
    Pure New Wool 143
    riding coat 102
    Russian and Bavarian uniform 41
    Russian mourning 189
    sanitary 142
    Shakespeare's father 73
    underwear 134, 142
Worth, Charles Frederick 183